UFO Initiation

Ultraterrestrial Time Travelers
Introduction

IDA M. KANNENBERG

Atlantis Phoenix
Missoula, Montana

Atlantis Phoenix
Missoula, Montana
AtlantisPhoenix.com

Order online at www.atlantisphoenix.com or email orders@atlantisphoenix.com. Quantity sales: Special discounts are available on quantity purchases by corporations, associations, and others.

First Edition

Copyright © Krsanna Duran 2013

ISBN 978-0615940830

Cover art by Hartmut Jager
Line drawings in Part II by Julie Wilkinson

Previously published as
UFOs and the Psychic Factor:
How to Understand Encounters with UFOs and ETs

This book is respectfully
dedicated to

Dr. R. Leo Sprinkle
of
Laramie, Wyoming

in sincere gratitude for his
much needed
encouragement, and for his
years of patience
in living through my miles
of wordage.

Ida M. Kannenberg

Other books by Ida M. Kannenberg

A SON OF OLD ATLANTIS

MY BROTHER IS A HAIRY MAN: THE SEARCH FOR BIGFOOT

PROJECT EARTH FROM THE ET PERSPECTIVE

TIME TRAVELERS FROM ATLANTIS

RECONCILIATION

THE ALIEN BOOK OF TRUTH: WHO AM I?
WHAT AM I DOING? WHY AM I HERE?

Contents

Foreword ~ Krsanna Duran i

Introduction ~ Leo R. Sprinkle, Ph.D. iii

Part I

Night of the Flaming Moon 1

Part II

Preface 25

Foreword 35

Chapters

One	The Process of Initiation	43
Two	Separation	57
Three	Round Enclosure	69
Four	Things and Symbols Seen	77
Five	Tutors	89
Six	Disciplines, Ordeals and Vows	99
Seven	Traditions: Cultural, Moral and Spiritual	113
Eight	Tasks	119
Nine	Revelations	125
Ten	Special Abilities	135
Eleven	Elevation	143
Twelve	Summary	151
Thirteen	Conclusion	155

Contents

Part III

Introduction to the Psychic World 161

Chapters

One   Psychic Essences Speak 163

Two   Resume on Psychic Essences 173

Three   Hallucinatory Events 183

Four   Psychic Manifestation 185

Five   Rmote Contact and Telepathy 187

Six   Remote Contact and Laser Beams 191

Seven   Electromagnetic Impulses 193

Eight   Sleep Learning 195

Nine   Observable Craft 197

Ten   Observable Occupants 199

Eleven   Purposes and Intent 201

Twelve   Total Organization 203

Thirteen   Future Expectations 207

Resources and Bibliography 213

Biography

Foreword

KRSANNA DURAN

In the process of discovering the nature of her UFO encounter in 1940, Ida Kannenberg worked with several groups: time travelers from Atlantis as well as extraterrestrials and non-physical spiritual mentors. Each cohort approached her with unique objectives and guidelines.

The son of an Atlantean time traveler and a Russian mother, Hweig[1] was a psychic master and instructor of psi who closely worked with Ida from 1968 to 1996. At various times he functioned in both terrestrial and ultraterrestrial modes. His time traveler grandparents took him to an Atlantean space island when he was seven, and then he was educated in Sirius. After returning to Earth in 1940, when he met Ida in a UFO contact, Hweig lived in San Francisco and Seattle.[2]

Ultraterrestrial visits from other dimensional realities that coexist in alternate time and space streams with ours are the basis of the interdimensional hypothesis (IDH) for UFOs. The IDH holds that UFOs are manifestations that have occurred throughout recorded history, but were ascribed to supernatural or mythological forces in prior ages. Today, they are usually regarded as a recent phenomenon, but, in fact, they are as ancient as our species.

The Time Travelers from Atlantis who contacted Ida Kannenberg drew a prime portrait of ultraterrestrial visitors that reside in the Earth's many dimensions. They have maintained contact with extraplanetary, or extraterrestrial, connections for millennia. In the real world of UFOs, both ultraterrestrials and extraterrestrials have been on the Earth since life began at the edge of the Milky Way. In the quest for interdimensional access to the cosmos, ultraterrestrials are on par with extraterrestrials. Both function with the knowledge of many dimensions of time and space, thus are capable of interdimensional movement.

---

[1] An Atlantean name pronounced *Hw-eye-jsh*.

[2] Kannenberg, Ida M. 2013. *A Son of Old Atlantis.* Missoula, MT: Letters 4 Earth

Before the planet's environment radically declined 13,000 years ago with genetic mutations in the Bigfoot species[3], both ultraterrestrials and extraterrestrials were openly present in human civilization. Civilization as we know it today emerged in a greatly impaired environment, which geologists identify with the beginning of the Holocene Age when numerous species became extinct.

A superwave from the galactic core generates a tsunami of change on the Earth about every 13,000 years, according to system theorist Paul LaViolette. The last superwave triggered the end of a major epoch 13,000 years ago, and the previous one 26,000 years ago coincided with the period that Edgar Cayce called the second destruction of Atlantis between 28,000 and 22,000 years ago. At the time of the second destruction, wars between factions of Atlanteans and Lemurians dominated the Earth. Several groups fled the social and environmental chaos in Atlantis approximately 22,000 years ago.

The time travelers who contacted Kannenberg moved through time to the present period. Alan, who contacted Daniel Fry at White Sands Missile Range in 1949, reported that his ancestors fled to Mars through space at the time of the last complete collapse of civilization, more than 100 generations in the past. The devastation of war and cataclysmic floods at the end of the last glacial period destroyed surface traces of Atlantis, but remnants of the Atlantean empire were embedded in early languages and cultures of modern civilization. Buried traces of that lost civilization preceding the modern world are being uncovered with deep explorations, recently further enabled with improved technology.

Several ultraterrestrial and extraterrestrial cohorts have periodically contacted the people of Earth since the third and final destruction of Atlantis approximately 12,000 years ago, after glacial flooding followed the last galactic superwave 13,000 years ago. Their capabilities to move through time and space, to disappear from sight as mysteriously as they appeared, endowed them with an aura of magic to the primitive civilization that had survived on Earth's surface.

Although from the same human root as modern humans, ultraterrestrials and extraterrestrials were viewed as supernaturals by primitive cultures. Those cosmic humans had retained technolog-

---

[3] Duran, Krsanna. 2013. *Planetary Web of Life and Cosmos: Human and Bigfoot Ancestors.* Missoula, Montana: Letters 4 Earth.

ical, social and spiritual sciences necessary for advanced civilizations.

In periodic visits they contacted individuals in various eras, and occasionally took contactees with them. Both Enoch, who traveled to the end of the Earth with the Lord, and Elijah, who disappeared in a beam of light, were "taken" in mysterious visits viewed as supernatural.

Initiations accompanied periodic appearances of apparently supernatural forces among the people of Earth. Knowledge needed for Earth's recovering civilization was imparted to contactees in processes of initiation. *Enoch* literally means *Initiator* in Hebrew. The *Book of Enoch* contains the first Hebraic treatise on astronomy, and the numbers of the Enochian calendar are embedded in ancient pyramids in Mexico at Teotihuacan. These are examined in *Planetary Web of Life and Cosmos: Human and Bigfoot Ancestors.*[4]

Initiation processes and symbols are vital keys for understanding both the ultra- and extraterrestrial contactors and objective of the contact. Secrets of the UFOs are embedded in symbols with roots in deep antiquity, bygone ages when ultraterrestrials lived among humans, which are commonly shown to contactees.

UFO contact cases commonly present elements of initiation that introduce novelty into the lives of contactees and, through them, into the larger social order in a process of slow-drip osmosis. Groundbreaking UFO investigator J. Allen Hynek chronicled extensive novelty in UFO cases as high strangeness that jolts the senses and awareness of observers. In the decades after Ida Kannenberg's 1940 encounter, initiation processes have been an identifying signature of ultra- and extraterrestrial UFO contact cases.

---

[4] Ibid.

Introduction

R. LEO SPRINKLE, PH.D.

Dear Reader: Prepare yourself for a treat! You are about to meet a charming and intelligent person: Ida M. Kannenberg. Mrs. Kannenberg is one of many persons who have experienced UFO encounters: thus, her experiences are not unique. However, her courage and commitment to truth are prominent among her personal qualities. She is a person who is willing to sharer knowledge so that you, or your friends and relatives, can consider the decision to step forward and add your own UFO report to that of thousands of other persons. If you were fortunate enough to meet Mrs. Kannenberg in person, you would see a tall, attractive woman with glasses: you would sense an open friendliness—and note a quiet, almost shy, manner of conducting herself in social situations. Rarely speaking until she has "something to say," she is impatient with "small talk" and eager to get on with the task at hand: gaining further knowledge about the mysteries of life on Earth and the possible connections between humankind and UFO phenomena.

Mrs. Kannenberg does not think of herself as a scholar or scientist: in fact, she sometimes describes herself as a "little old lady in tennis shoes." Like most UFO abductees or contactees, she sees herself as an unobtrusive, unimportant, "everyday" person. However, she shows the intelligence, the dedication, the attention to detail, and the internal and external awareness that characterize the creative artist/scientist. Further, she is willing to mask her social shyness in order to share her view of the UFO message with other interested persons.

The message that Ida has received from her UFO mentors is simple: UFO people have come to rejuvenate the Earth and to assist humankind in their evolutionary development. However, there is difficulty in spreading the message! (I am reminded of the hero in the movie, "Oh God!," starring John Denver and George Burns. The hero is told by God to tell other people: (1) God exists; (2) be kind to one another. The message is simple; however, the task is difficult:

convincing other people, especially learned professors, that God has chosen a simple person to deliver a simple message!) Ida is aware of the many questions that surround the UFO mystery; in fact, she describes vividly her own doubts and fears about the reality of her experiences, as well as the anxieties and worries about telling her relatives and friends of her experiences. Like most UFO observers, she found it easier—at first—to minimize or to "forget" her UFO experience. Later, her basic honesty and stubbornness forced her to recognize the reality of the experience, and the need to accept herself as a "contactee."

UFO contactees should be fascinating persons, from the viewpoint of the professional psychologist. However, there have been few long range, formal studies of UFO contactees. Thus, what we know of them comes from small surveys, or individual case studies. Few behavioral scientists have ventured into the uncharted areas of UFO phenomena; however, more and more social scientists are joining physical and biological scientists in the investigation of UFO reports.

My professional interest in UFO observers and UFO contactees was sparked by my own UFO experiences: a 1949 sighting of a "flying saucer," or daylight disc, which was moving over the campus of the University of Colorado-Boulder; a fellow college student, Joe Waggoner, and I discussed our observation of the object, but I didn't wish to discuss the sighting with others. Prior to the incident, I knew that "only kooks see UFOs." I had been a "scoffer" or a "believer" in the non-reality of "flying saucers"; however, after the sighting, I became a "skeptic," because I could not explain the observation.

In 1956, my wife, Marilyn, and I observed a "nocturnal light" that moved, hovered, moved and hovered, between us and the "Flatirons" (Rocky Mountain foothills), near Boulder, Colorado; after the second UFO sighting, I changed from a "skeptic" to a "believer" in the reality of UFOs—whatever they might be.

Now, as a result of hypnotic sessions that have helped me to recall some unusual childhood memories, I consider myself to be among those persons who are UFO **"contactees"—persons who feel as if they have a "task" or a "mission" or a "duty" to assist their fellow humans to prepare for the UFO message.**

When I finished doctoral studies at the University of Missouri in 1961, I had two professional daydreams: to contribute to the field of counseling psychology, and to learn more about the personal characteristics of UFO observers. I joined the Department of Psychology at the University of North Dakota-Grand Forks, and I was impressed with my colleagues; most of them were "young Turks," who were "going places," and they were excellent teachers and researchers. However, one day a colleague chided me: "Leo! What the hell are you doing? Looking into ESP, hypnosis and UFO reports! You'll lose any reputation you might earn later!" I found myself at the decision point: did I see myself as a professor and a contributor to "science," or did I see myself as a professor and an investigator of UFO reports? I decided that I must follow the path of UFO investigation, even if it meant to others that I could not be viewed as a "real" scientist.

I joined NICAP (National Investigations Committee of Aerial Phenomena). Richard Hall assisted me in conducting a survey of NICAP members and comparing their level of "dogmatism" (Rokeach Dogmatism Scale) with that of a sample of graduate students and professors of psychology.

I became a consultant to APRO (Aerial Phenomena Research Organization), and I learned much from Jim and Coral Lorenzen about their early UFO investigations. I moved in 1964 to the University of Wyoming, and I enjoyed the opportunity to meet the Lorenzens in person during their vacation travels. They encouraged my interest in the psychological characteristics of UFO observers and the experiences of UFO abductees. In 1966, a New York TV program (with John G. Fuller, J. Allen Hynek, Donald H. Menzel, and Frank Salisbury) was as exciting as participating in my first hypnotic time regression session with a person who claimed an encounter with a "flying saucer." Then, during a New York TV program with Betty and Barney Hill (who were being interviewed by the late James McDonald, Carl Sagan, two science writers, and myself), I was fascinated to observe that the UFO abductees were not only intelligent but also just as self-aware and self-accepting as the skeptical professors and science writers! I began to wonder if other UFO abductees were as charming, sincere, and open as Betty and Barney Hill.

In 1963-64, I began a survey of persons who claim to experience UFO phenomena; my hope was to obtain a sample of 100 persons—in one year—and learn more about their characteristics and their claims of dreams, visions, poltergeist activity, obsessions and compulsions, and mental communication with UFO occupants. It took four years to obtain results from 83 participants. The results were gratifying: Most participants were "normal" in their responses to standardized personality inventories.

Now, in 1992, there are many studies of UFO experiences, including the 1986 Parnell Study of 225 participants (Dr. June Parnell's dissertation study at the University of Wyoming). Each year, since 1980, the Rocky Mt. Conference on UFO Investigation ("contactee conference") has been held on the campus of the University of Wyoming in Laramie. (See the article by James S. Gordon, M.D., in the August, 1991, issue of *The Atlantic Monthly.)* The conference serves as a forum for UFO contactees and UFO researchers to meet and to share their mutual suspicions and interests.

Studies of UFO experiencers have led me to the tentative conclusion that the majority of them are "normal" in their psychological functioning; however, many of them seem to be frightened and emotionally upset by their encounters with UFO entities. Training in counseling techniques, and willingness to describe one's own UFO experiences, seems to assist UFO abductees as they allow themselves to "go through" the fear and anger of reliving their UFO abductions during hypnotic sessions. Many of these persons report a reduction of anxiety and anguish as a result of their decision to "accept" the reality of their UFO experiences.

At first, many UFO experiencers explain their memories of UFO encounters as impressions based upon "dreams," "fantasies," "imagination," "crazy ideas," "fears" or "overeating." From the viewpoint of this UFO investigator, it seems that UFO contactees are "allowed" to think of their experiences in any way that they choose: dream, fantasy, out-of-body experience or face-to-face physical encounter with UFOLKS. However, the important effect seems to be a "programming" effect: the UFO contactee begins to respond to an internal "suggestion," "wish," "desire," "need," "obsession" and/or "compulsion" to engage in a special task or mission. Conscious awareness of the UFO experience may arise later, after the "task" is "completed."

The dilemma of non-belief in UFOs versus the belief in UFOs goes on and on. As J. Allen Hynek pointed out in his 1979 lecture in Brasilia, Brazil, theoretical physicists have lived for many years with the dilemma of light: light can be viewed as reacting like particles, and light can be viewed as reacting like waves. Hynek went on to ask, rhetorically: If the physicist can accept the dilemma of light-as-particles and light-as-waves, then cannot the

UFO investigator accept the dilemma of UFOs-as-objects and UFOs-as-psychic events?

Some UFO investigators prefer to be "impaled" on the horn of UFOs as objects, thinking that "flying saucers" come from other planets and hoping that other nations are better enemies than ghosts and goblins. Other UFO investigators prefer to be "impaled" on the horn of UFOs as psychic events, thinking that UFOs arise from our "collective unconscious" or archetypal forces, and hoping that poltergeists and psychic forces are more acceptable as masters than extraterrestrial beings. Is the "psychic" hypothesis correct? Is the "object" hypothesis correct? Are both hypotheses correct? Or, is it possible that the problem is more difficult than either of these two groups have imagined: is it possible that humankind must learn to serve a harsher master than psychic forces or extraterrestrial entities? Must we seek our own spiritual destiny, to use our own intellectual awareness, to control our own emotional reactions, to learn our role as caretakers of the Earth and to become Cosmic Citizens?

These general questions cannot be answered on the basis of individual UFO claims; however, it is interesting to note that many individual UFO contactees find themselves worrying about these same questions. Prior to their UFO encounters, their concerns usually seem to be of everyday matters such as family, education, job and the high cost of living. After their UFO encounters, they seem to experience an increase of worry, doubt, anxiety, and fear-including the fear of "going crazy." Their dilemma increases as they anguish over the question of "keeping quiet" or "telling" someone about their doubts, fears and the events that have occurred.

And now, as I promised you earlier, here is Ida M. Kannenberg. Let her take you with her as she describes her own questions and her own doubts—her personal journey into the UFO experience. As you read of her experiences, listen to your "inner self"; what parts of her experience are similar to your experiences? What events are different? What do these events mean to you?

If you have experienced a similar UFO encounter, or similar psychic events, are you willing to describe your experiences to interested persons and to UFO investigative organizations? Do you have enough honesty, courage and strength to share with others who are willing to describe their UFO experiences? Perhaps your answer will be "Yes"; perhaps your answer will be "No"; perhaps your answer will be "Not Now." So be it. In any event, I suggest that you sit back and enjoy your own interpretation of the significance and meaning of the UFO story.

Dear reader, I am pleased to introduce you to Mrs. Ida M. Kannenberg.

Part I

The Night of the Flaming Moon

It has taken me fifty years to bring this event to memory, to recall and check details, particularly dates and times, to piece it all together and even begin to comprehend.

To put us all in a proper mood, I shall call this

The Night of the Flaming Moon...

In December, 1940, my husband and I were living in Bremerton, Washington. I had already mailed my Christmas presents to my sister, her family and my parents. So I was greatly surprised when my husband phoned about 2:30 in the afternoon of December 20th, and said, "Can you be ready to leave at midnight for Phoenix?"

"Sure," I said, "But how come?"

"It will be a share-the-expense trip with a young man going to Austin, Texas, to be married. He has to be there by Christmas Eve. There will also be two servicemen in the car, so you can take only one small suitcase."

So long ago! I do not remember all the details, but I know I was ready and waiting at the designated time. We left Bremerton "at the head of the bay" just as the time slid past midnight, going into the 21st.

The other passengers were a young Navy man, who would leave us in Los Angeles to join his ship farther south, and a young Army fellow. The driver had taken his Air Force training and would enter the service after his honeymoon.

The first part of the trip was rough and scary, with heavy rains, dim lights and winding mountainous roads. All the while we were trying to "make time" to get our driver to his wedding on time. We stopped only for rest stops, to eat and to get gas.

In Los Angeles, however, the Navy man left us and we had to wait about three hours while the car was serviced. We had come through a bad dust storm near Bakersfield, and the men agreed that some vital things should be done before heading east over the desert at night.

We pulled out of Los Angeles between 5:00 and 5:30 p.m. in the afternoon of December 22nd. We seemed to crawl through the maze of little towns and hamlets out of Los Angeles. After Riverside the traffic cleared and we could make better time. It had rained heavily though intermittently, and we had some hesitations about crossing low spots due to surging water.

Sketch from memory of the relative positions of the car as the "full moon" sidled out to the left of the rock and became a "rea ball."

It was quite chilly, and I was thankful for the blanket that I wrapped tightly about me as I tried to doze.

Several times through the hills we saw small spotty fires, started no doubt by the energetic lightning, little beginnings of forest fires, none of which looked very threatening.

At Indio we stopped at a little cafe for a rest stop, a piece of apple pie and coffee. As we left the cafe, I glanced at my watch and said to myself, "9:20. I must remember this time." And then, "That's silly! Why would I want to remember the time?"

Somewhere beyond Indio I awoke with a start, stretched as much as possible, and sat up. We were just rounding a corner over a little hill. Over the valley before us was seeping a deep red, unearthly glow.

"What's that?" one of the men cried, startled, as indeed I was also.

The glow seeped slowly up the sides of the mountains in the background and the hills on either side of the valley. It was weird, spooky, almost menacing.

"Another forest fire," someone suggested, but it did not look at all like the fires we had seen earlier. The glow was too deep, too even, too red, a blood-red glow that soon permeated the whole area.

"That's not fire!"

Then on the horizon, between the two ranges of distant hills, an elliptical form appeared, intensely burning red.

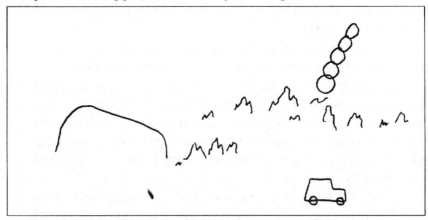

As we started on, the silvery white disk rose rapidly at a slight angle. Sketch made from memory.

"Oh, it's only the full moon coming up," I cried, greatly relieved. "It always looks weird on the desert, so huge and red."

But the elliptical form appeared to be coming toward us, not rising into the rounded form of a moon. The car was going so fast and the glow was so brilliant that it was difficult to determine just what the movement actually was. It just seemed to grow and grow and come closer and closer. I had grown up on the desert at Tucson and had seen many a moonrise, but never like this! It had obliterated the lines of hills to the left of us. It appeared almost as though it was in front of the hills! Why didn't it stay on the horizon where it belonged?

Suddenly, right there, our view was cut off by a hill. We kept staring, expecting to see the moon rise over the top of the hill. Instead it began to move sideways.

"That can't be the moon," I cried. "It's coming out sideways!" As it came it rounded out like a huge ball.

The road made a sharp turn. The bend was very wide, and the driver pulled off to the left side of the road in the bend and stopped. There were scrubby trees and bushes alongside the road and now we could no longer see the red glow.

The driver touched my husband on the shoulder and said to the Army man in back, "Come on."

The three went down the road and stood, out of my hearing, heads bent together, talking and talking and talking.

"What can they be talking about so long?" I wondered a bit petulantly. It was cold, and we were all exceedingly tired. I wanted to keep going.

I looked at my watch. It was twenty minutes to an hour, which I later determined was twelve. Still the men talked.

I wadded up in my blanket again and tried to doze. Once I stirred, as I thought I heard the crunch of footsteps in the gravel. I thought the back door opened and a blast of cold air hit me. I vaguely wondered why no one was saying anything and why only one door opened, but then I was not aware of anything more.

Presently I again sat up and yawned, feeling quite peevish. The men were still in the headlights talking. I looked at my watch. It was twenty minutes past midnight. I snapped the light on in the top of the car to see better. "I must have looked at my watch wrong before," I thought. "They simply could not have been talking this long!"

Again I heard the scuffle of footsteps and I thought sleepily, "I thought the fellows came back once before. I must have dreamed it." The men had now returned to the car, remarking about how cold it was.

The young Army corporal, who had been riding in back with me, ran ahead of the older men and climbed into the back exclaiming, "If I had known we would be out there this long, I would have worn my jacket."

His teeth were chattering, and he was shaking. He donned his service jacket and curled down on the floor of the car. I gave him my blanket, as I wore a heavy wrap-around plaid coat that I had bought specially for the trip. We would be going home on the Greyhound through Utah just after New Year's.

My husband Dave and the driver, whom I remember as Tom, conferred as to the time we had stopped and when they had returned to the car. They decided it had to be between forty-five minutes to an hour and sounded amazed that it had been so long. They concluded that the next truck stop would be in Blythe, where we might get hot coffee to warm up.

As we drove away, there was a great white silvery disk rising obliquely in the sky, just over the tree tops.

"You see," someone said, "it was only the moon rising!"

"But it's going so fast," I argued. "It's just shooting up!" It had risen from about thirty degrees elevation to sixty degrees in less than a minute.

"It only looks that way because we are going in the same direction."

I started to argue, "But it is going *up.* We are not going *up.*" But I had argued enough.

It still did not seem like a true moonrise to me. Where had it been lurking the forty minutes that I was asleep? Actually it must have been well over an hour from the time we had first seen the moonrise until we saw it again over the tree tops. It should have been high in the sky by this time.

I do not remember that I left the car when they stopped at Blythe for coffee. I know I felt totally exhausted.

Again I dozed, and again I awoke about two hours later. High above us in a now clear sky hung a quarter moon.

"Look!" I said. "There's the real moon. It's only a quarter moon!" No one said anything for a moment. Then my husband said, "Clouds are hiding part of it."

I looked and looked. There were no clouds obscuring the moon. It was absolutely and definitely a quarter moon!

We reached my sister's house in Phoenix about 4:30 a.m. Both my sister and my niece, who was twelve years old, remember us talking about the strange red light.

The next day I found my husband sitting alone in the living room. He seemed to be thinking deeply, and I asked, "What did you men talk about when you got out of the car and stood so long in the headlights last night?"

He looked at me questioningly. "We didn't get out of the car," he said.

"Yes, you did, all three of you. And you stood in the cold talking for a long, long time. I don't want to know the details, just tell me the subject that was so vital to discuss out of my hearing."

"Oh nothing," he said, "nothing important."

For some reason I then completely forgot about the strange moonrise. It absolutely washed out of my mind. I never thought of it for nearly twenty years. When someone mentioned UFOs, I suddenly remembered the great, glowing red ball and wondered, "could that have been a UFO?" In 1968, I began to hear interior voices. At that time I did not recall the UFO incident, or anything that had been told to me. Three of the voice owners, who claimed UFO connection, Hweig, Amorto, and Jamie, tried to convince me that everything was just fine and no harm would come to me. Another refused to give any name, so I called him The Hidden One.

Things became rather fun until some malevolent voices broke in, teasing and tormenting. I was thoroughly terrorized. I sought psychiatric help, which was not very helpful.

One day as the tormenting ones were quite frightening, a powerful voice spoke interiorly. "Leave this woman alone!" There was silence, then a rustling little whisper, "Ida, who are you?"

"Just Ida," I whispered back. "That is all I know."

The commanding voice reverberated again in my head, "Leave this woman alone!"

There were no more voices for nine years. In November, 1977, my old unseen but talkative comrades returned, Hweig, Amorto, and Jamie. They said that they had learned how to protect me from unwanted invasion. One or the other, and occasionally. The Hidden One also, has been in contact ever since. I suspect it was he who commanded the nasties to leave.

In 1979, I read a story in a magazine about alien voices, written by Dr. Leo Sprinkle. I wrote to him describing my plight. His answer was so friendly and understanding that we continue our correspondence to this day. I must admit the advent of UFOs into my life has given me some welcome and treasured friendships, both seen and unseen.

In 1980, I checked on that full moonrise of December 22-23, 1940. I obtained the phases of the moon for that month and year, and I found that the full moon could have been observed rising on December 14th. On December 23rd, the phase of the moon should have been the quarter, just as we had seen the second moon the same night.

I began to wonder about that forty minutes I had been "asleep" while the men stood in the road talking.

I decided the time had come for hypnotic regression, and I traveled to Laramie, Wyoming, to Dr. R. Leo Sprinkle for that purpose. What follows is an entry in my journal two weeks before by regression:

April 5, 1980

Today I received a letter from another contactee with a paragraph that had been delivered to her by the UFOLK, as Dr. Leo calls them. They spoke of wanting to strengthen our race with their intelligence through mental telepathy and interbreeding of genes. "This has been achieved by mind transfer at the birth of one of your children, through this transfer we then have contact with the occupant and when the child reaches an age for mental development we then begin instructions," etc.

Just the day before I had written another contactee who wanted to know if my hypnosis session with Dr. Leo was to be about UFO business only. I told her I wanted to be regressed to my birth scene.

I was born the second of twins, a blue baby and pronounced dead at birth by a somewhat inebriated doctor. He wrapped me in a blanket and told my father to dispose of "it."

After all else was tended to and the doctor gone, my maternal grandmother unwrapped the expired one (me)—and gave me mouth to mouth resuscitation. Here I am. I have always wondered if I am really I or some secondary attempt at life.

Amorto told me once I was not a "Star People" but a "Something Else." Can these "Something Else's" of which I am supposed to be one, be a mind transfer? Is that why these fellows have asked me over and over, "Ida, who are you?" Perhaps I should try to find the answer to this at the hypnosis session on April 19th.

On June 24th the communicators said, "We laugh at you for what you are! You are the one who now becomes the interpreter."

And on July 29, 1979, Hweig mentioned that a particular type of personality came into the world to interact with the UFO people, adding strangely, "It all lies dormant in your mind."

Am I then a Mind Transfer? —Ida.

In the following presentation of my first hypnosis session of April 19, 1980, hypnotic procedures as used by Dr. R. Leo Sprinkle have been minimally retained. Other material has been very slightly edited to delete repetitious, clumsy or obscure words. Other than these very few and very minor changes, the transcript renders the original recording precisely-

HYPNOSIS SESSION OF APRIL 19, 1980

University of Wyoming, Laramie

Dr. S.: I am Leo Sprinkle. I serve as director of Counseling and Testing at the University of Wyoming, and today we are filming a session with Mrs. Ida M. Kannenberg. Accompanying her is her daughter, Mrs. Lee Crawley. Also we have with us as cameraman, and all around good man of many talents, Michael Lewis, who is filming. Our purpose here is to interview Ida Kannenberg and with hypnotic techniques see what we can determine about some early experiences in her life and whether they have some connection with more recent events concerning information that she is gaining. So we'll turn to Ida and ask what information she would like to see if we can determine today. What things would be useful for us to explore?

Ida: Well, the first thing I would like to know is whether the object we saw on the California desert in 1940 could have been a UFO? We thought at that time that it was a full moon rising, but since then we have checked the dates, and the full moon arose a good ten days before we saw this object. And also later that same night we saw a quarter moon in the same sky, and that doesn't quite add up.

Dr. S.: O.K. So one question is: What happened on that December, 1940, incident...and another topic?

Ida: I've been told that when I was a little girl about seven and a half years old, I was playing under a lilac tree, and two men approached. All that I can remember is that they asked me where a certain person lived in that neighborhood, which I was able to tell them. However, they did not go to his house. Later they got into their car and drove off down the street.

Now my present communicators tell me that at the same time the two men told me (I supposed subconsciously or in some fashion I did not hear) that I was to study people, to learn to write well, and that someday they would see me again...I think they also told me to be a good girl.

Dr. S.: That sounds appropriate, I suppose. O.K. Learn to write well and to study people, and they would meet you again someday, or talk to you?

Ida: Yes.

Dr. S.: So that is another incident that would be useful to explore in terms of memories with hypnotic procedures. Another topic?

Ida: There is some question of the time when I was born. I was pronounced dead by the doctor and it was a good half hour later before someone took pains to revive me, and I just wonder how this could be possible. I was a blue baby, and there are some factors there I would like to see brought out through hypnosis.

Dr. S: O.K. We'll follow along on that same sequence. Let's practice relaxation procedures, and then when we're ready, we will go back to that December '40 incident.

(Adjusts chair, then goes into hypnotic procedures.)

Dr. S: Feeling pleasant and comfortable now, ready for the journey?

Ida: Yes.

Dr. S: Drifting back, back through time. And now you will be able to talk and describe your impressions. What are you experiencing now?

Ida: Nothing.

Dr. S.: Nothing happening right now?

Ida: No.

Dr. S: O.K. Just let yourself relax...let yourself be aware at what point you'd like to begin the journey.

Ida: Just going over the hill and seeing the light.

Dr. S.: O.K. You're going over the hill and seeing the light. Talk and describe what happens next.

Ida: I'm just not there!

Dr. S: You don't feel yourself there at that point. Is there something else that we need to understand or to deal with first? Is there something missing?

Ida: No.

Dr. S.: Did something happen earlier in the journey?

Ida: No.

Dr. S.: Now just back up a bit in your memory. Go back to the time when you first started out on your journey. What was the purpose...when did you begin?

Ida: It was very unexpected. My husband just called about 2:30 in the afternoon and said, "We're leaving at midnight for Arizona." We lived in Bremerton, Washington then. We were going to Phoenix to my sister's house. My folks would meet us there and then take us down to their mine. He said to be ready by midnight. And we were driving with a young fellow who was going to Austin, Texas, to be married. It was his car. There was another younger man, a sailor, who got off in Los Angeles. And then there was another man, I think he was Army.

Dr. S.: So you drive from Washington state down to San Diego?

Ida: Los Angeles.

Dr. S.: Los Angeles. Then you drive east over the desert toward Arizona. O.K. And nothing seems to be unusual except the unexpected timing of the trip.

Ida: No, that was all. It was a very quick trip. We didn't stop for anything except, of course, to eat and get gas. Drove straight through.

Dr. S.: So then the question mark is when you are driving up over the hill and you see the round glow or the round light?

Ida: Yes. There was a deep red light. We had passed several forest fires and we thought perhaps at first that this was another forest fire but it wasn't the right color; it was too deep a red and too even. There weren't just flames. There was a completely even red glow through the valley...

Dr. S.: So there is some conscious recollection of the events, but the feeling is you are not there yet in terms of experiencing it again.

Ida: That's right.

Dr. S.: Well, let's go back and see if we can pick up impressions of an earlier time. Just relax deeply...allow yourself to go to a time and place that may be more related or in some way connected with this desert experience. Let yourself drift back in time. Perhaps it is the seven-year-old experience. Perhaps it is the time of birth, perhaps it is some other time. Feel yourself going deeper and deeper, closer and closer to that time and the experience that is significant and meaningful to you and that has deep reverberations in your subconscious mind regarding these events and any connection between these events. You are there now. What is happening now?

Ida: Nothing.

Dr. S.: Nothing. Any feelings or thoughts come into your mind?

Ida: No.

Dr. S.: Feeling relaxed and comfortable but just not any...

Ida: Feeling relaxed and comfortable and just right here.

Dr. S.: Um-Hum. O.K. Where would you like to be if you allowed yourself to go to a time and place that is significant? Where would you like to go?

Ida: Egypt.

Dr. S.: Let yourself go to Egypt...let yourself go in your imagination. If you want to think of it as a real trip, fine. If you want to think of it as an out-of-body experience, if you want to think of it as a fantasy or day dream, it doesn't matter. The important thing is to just let yourself drift up and away out of the chair...on the way to places in Egypt that you'd like to visit. What happens as you see yourself drifting in that direction?

Ida: I think I'm a complete dud.

Dr. S.: That takes a lot of practice to be a complete dud.

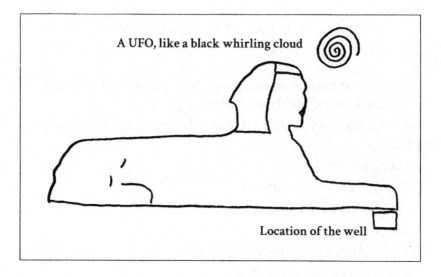

The Sphinx.5 A chamber beneath the paws of the Sphinx was discovered by geologist Dr. Robert Schoch during a 1999 study. Located between the two paws, the chamber partially extends under the right paw when the Sphinx is viewed from the front. The area had not been excavated to determine the presence of a well near the chamber, as of 2013.

Ida: I'm just right here.

---

5 Schoch, Robert Dr. 2005. *Pyramid Quest.* Strand, London, England: Penguin Books Ltd.

Dr. S.: Yes, your body is right here, but what is happening in your imagination?

Ida: A perfect blank.

Dr. S.: That takes some skill to get a perfect blank. What would happen if you did go to Egypt? What would you like to visit?

Ida: The sphinx.

Dr. S.: Can you picture the sphinx?

Ida: Yes.

Dr. S.: O.K. Picture the sphinx, and see what direction you would like to approach the sphinx. Where would you like to set down?

Ida: I'm approaching toward the right paw at an oblique angle.

Dr. S.: And what do you anticipate when you set down? Are you going to set down in a particular spot, a particular place?

Ida: The closest place to me on the right paw. That's the outer corner, I guess you'd call it, of the right paw.

Dr. S.: Just let yourself set down there and see what happens next.

(Long pause.)

Ida: I'm afraid it faded out.

Dr. S.: Do you see yourself inside?

Ida: No.

Dr. S.: Above or below the sphinx?

Ida: I'm walking toward it.

Dr. S.: What happens next?

Ida: It keeps fading away again.

Dr. S.: Anything come in its place?

Ida: No.

Dr. S.: Any feeling you've been there before?

Ida: No. But it's important to go.

Dr. S.: O.K. Just let yourself go ahead and see what you experience next.

(Long pause)

Ida: Something deep. I have to go very, very deep.

Dr. S.: Let yourself go deeper and deeper...allow it to happen, whatever it is. Allow the memories to flow through you...

(Long pause)

Ida: There's a UFO.

Dr. S.: There's a UFO—where do you see a UFO?

Ida: Coming over by the head...to the left of the head. To my right.

Dr. S.: How does it appear?

Ida: Dark like a cloud. Like a whirling cloud. There's a message.

Dr. S.: And can you interpret the message?

Ida: Something is to be found. Deep. They look in the wrong place. They have said it is the left paw. Someone looked, described it wrong. It's the right paw.

Dr. S.: Do you have an impression of what this something is?

Ida: Cayce said records of Atlantis. That's not it...something about water...well.

Dr. S.: Well. Let yourself focus in on it, what it is. So you'll be able to gain more impressions about what it is.

Ida: Skeletons...very deep....very, very deep.

Dr. S.: Any impressions of how deep? In feet or yards?

Ida: Maybe 200 feet. Maybe not quite.

Dr. S.: Maybe 200 feet below the right paw of the sphinx?

Ida: At the side and deep...not directly below

Dr. S.: At the side and deep. O.K. Any other impressions about what is there?

Ida: The well...dangerous...underground water could be dangerous.

Dr. S.: Dangerous in the sense of...?

Ida: Flooding while working.

Dr. S.: Any other impressions about the area or about the message?

Ida: No. Just things I've read interfere.

Dr. S.: Yes, it is hard to know what is memory and what is an impression of the area. Do you see the message in some kind of written form or paper form?

Ida: Telepathy.

Dr. S.: Any impression of how many skeletons are there?

Ida: Very few, two, three

Dr. S.: And an impression about what happened causing the skeletons to be buried there?

Ida: Murder!

Dr. S.: Murder! By whom? For what purpose?

Ida: Priests.

Dr. S.: These are skeletons of priests...or they're...

Ida: No. Priests murdered them.

Dr. S.: Any impression of who was murdered and why?

Ida: People from the other UFO. Priests jealous. Afraid of new religion, destroy them.

Dr. S.: So the priests were afraid these people represented a threat to them, the possibility of a new religion, so this is why they killed the UFO people?

Ida: That's right. It will happen again.

Dr. S.: Any impressions of where it will happen again, or when it will happen again?

Ida: Same general area. Time not available. When other events occur...events synchronize. No calendar, clock time.

Dr. S.: I see. Do you have an impression of what these other events will be?

Ida: War. Threat of atomic war. Never come to pass. They will interfere. That area.

Dr. S.: Any other impressions of events that are related?

Ida: Someone wants to speak through my voice!

Dr. S.: O.K. Fine. You can allow someone to speak through your voice.

Ida: (Deep, heavy voice) War will not be tolerated. It endangers all, other planets, other peoples. Millions. Millions of people. It will be stopped by psychic means, not weapons. Many are ready to help. They know not what they are to do now. They will be told. That is all. Later I speak again. Later. Now the other events may be told.

Dr. S.: All right. Thank you.

Ida: (as though to self) You may rest. (Comes out of hypnosis.)

Dr. S.: How did that feel to you?

Ida: He (Hweig) said it was going to happen, (clears throat)

Dr. S.: Did you anticipate what would be said when you knew that there would be another message?

Ida: No, I had no idea what it was to be.

Dr. S.: War will not be tolerated!

Ida: How do you not tolerate one war unless you have another war to not tolerate the first war?

Dr. S.: Good question!

Ida: By psychic means, he said.

(Short rest.)

Ida: O.K. We're ready.

Dr. S.: This time looks like we're ready to relax and go back to the experiences. Had to get the introduction first.

Ida: Somebody had to get his two bits' worth in first.

Dr. S.: Right. When you're ready, just lean back and relax. Back to the 1940 incident in December. Feel yourself be there vividly and accurately, and be able to describe your impressions and the events of that particular day and that particular night...feeling relaxed and comfortable now?

Ida: Yes.

Dr. S.: What feeling or thought is paramount about that incident?

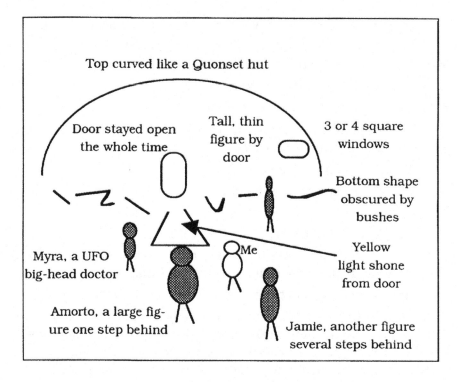

Top curved like a Quonset hut

Door stayed open the whole time

Tall, thin figure by door

3 or 4 square windows

Bottom shape obscured by bushes

Myra, a UFO big-head doctor

Me

Yellow light shone from door

Amorto, a large figure one step behind

Jamie, another figure several steps behind

Entering the cabin.

Ida: Strange.

Dr. S.: Strange. Seems strange. O.K. Just focus on that feeling of strangeness....what comes to mind when you focus on that feeling of something being strange?

Ida: Presence...presence of someone...can't review it visually. Can remember...some.

Dr. S.: Some. O.K.

Ida: Not forest fire. Too deep, too red, too even. Just even glow, red at first, very dark red, then the round shape comes from behind big rock, out to left. I must see it visually to continue...

Dr. S.: O.K. Be aware when it is appropriate, when you are ready you will be able to see it visually. Focusing on that strangeness, on that red spot...picture yourself viewing it. Let's see what happens next.

Ida: (sighing) Too much interference.

Dr. S.: Interference? Thoughts or feelings?

Ida: Presence.

Dr. S.: Just ask the presence if it is all right if you review these events. Ask for permission to review these events and see what happens then.

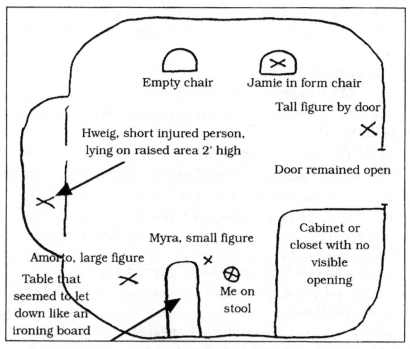

Inside the cabin.

Ida: "Are you gonna let me see this or not?"

Dr. S.: What's the verdict?

Ida: Not yet...something forgotten...who forgot? (Pause) They forgot.

Dr. S.: Something that has to be remembered first before we can be able to go back to this? Do they say what they forgot?

Ida: Subconscious closed. They use superconscious.

Dr. S.: Can they give permission to open up the subconscious?

Ida: No. Lets other entities in. Interference. Dangerous.

Dr. S.: But if we open up that information while protected, is that possible?

Ida: Not enough protection. Superconscious can be used.

Dr. S.: O.K. Is permission given for superconscious to be used? To recall?

Ida: Yes.

Dr. S.: Let yourself use the superconscious level of awareness to recall the events as you're watching the round red spot. What happens next?

Ida: We stop side of road. Left side. Men go down road. Front of car. Headlights. Stay long, long, long time. I think I'll rest. Doze.

(Long pause)

Dr. S.: What happens as the body dozes?

Ida: Who are you? (Voice strong but quivery, as though held steady by effort.)

Dr. S.: Are you speaking to me?

Ida: No, I speak to someone. Them. I'm frightened.

Dr. S.: You speak to someone and you're frightened?

Ida: Two. They need help. Ask me for help...very disturbed themselves...come help. I can't visualize this. I only remember. Jamie, another figure several steps behind three or four square windows Top curved like a Quonset hut

Dr. S.: But you do remember the impressions? O.K. Let the impressions flow.

Ida: I ask what kind of help. Problem—what problem? Someone hurt, needs blood transfusion. I say my type might not work. They say they know my type. It's O.K. It is a rare type. They are almost frantic themselves. I forget to be afraid. I go with them. Round cabin. I think cabin. (Changed tape here and lost some words.) Inside light. Everything white metal. Sit on high stool. Left arm. Take blood. Big syringe? (questioningly)

Dr. S.: Like syringe?

Ida: Yes. One—two—three—four—five men...look like us. One injured, bleeding. Chest. Shorter than others, covered blanket. Can't see much. Blanket metal too! (wonderingly)

Dr. S.: Blanket is metal?

Ida: They ask help other ways. Want to communicate again. Press something into my ears. Way in, hurts. My nose, left nostril. Can't see. Way up, way, way up, hurts, not too bad. Can't see features. Can't remember. Taller than I, but look like us, human like us. Only one speaks to me. Others look at each other, nod, seem to talk—know—without speaking. One speaks to me. English. No accent. They tell me saved his life. Many thanks. They contact much later to help again. Vaguely see. Very, very vaguely. Nothing clear. More impressions than sight. Some sight. Take me back car. Later I look at watch. Think I've been asleep forty minutes. Decide I looked at watch wrong first time, couldn't be that long. Fellows come back to car. We see quarter moon in sky, half way between quarter moon and new moon. So the big round red thing we saw before—how could there be two moons? Doesn't make sense.

Ida in her scout uniform, under the lilac tree. Photo taken by her Mother in May 1922.

Dr. S.: O.K. Doing well. Just relax deeply...be aware that later on we'll have more information about these impressions as expressed...now allow yourself to go back to the time during childhood...about your experience that may have occurred around seven years of age...of talking with, meeting with some strange men. See what impressions come to mind.

Ida: I am going down Carey Avenue.

Dr. S.: You're going down where?

Ida: Carey Avenue. We live there in Davenport, Iowa. I am going home. There were no violets to pick. Only garter snakes. Maybe there are some lilacs left, but I don't like to go over where they are. But I will go. I will take my mother some lilacs. There weren't any violets. They're gone. Too late. I don't like to be here, (sigh) But I think I will sit under the bush awhile. No, I'll lie down. I like to hear the ground. I think I'll go to sleep a little. But someone is coming. I hear footsteps in the grass, so I sit up. I didn't wear my glasses to play, so I can't see too well. Two men. One, big man, gray hair. One younger man, smaller. Business men, business suits. Probably rich men.

They ask me, "Do you know Mr. Barton?" (as a question to self.)

"Mr. Barton."

"Yes, the blind man."

"Doesn't he live around here somewhere?"

"Right there. That house."

"This one right here?"

"Yes"

They talk together, I can't hear. Can't understand because I can't hear too clearly. Mumble. The older man speaks again to me. The younger man speaks only to him.

"What is your name? Where do you live? What does your father do?"

It is hard to remember. What is he saying?

"Where do you go to school? Do you like school?"

Why do they always ask that! He says something, but I don't hear him. He's saying it like inside my head.

"You will need to know all about people, why they do what they do. Why they act as they do, what do they mean besides what they say? You will learn to write well; try harder at your spelling. Learn about grammar. Make nice sentences. Someday you will write many wonderful unknown things. We will see you again when you are grown up and much older." Then he says out loud, "Be a good girl."

They always say that, too. They go away to their car. It's parked on the wrong side of the street. They must not know they can't park on that side of the street. Then they drive away. They don't go to Mr. Barton's house.

I start home and meet my mother coming. She has her camera. She says, "Who were the men talking to you?" I told her what I knew they said. She said, "I just wondered." She said, "I have one picture left. I want to take it so I can send them to be finished." So we went back to the lilac tree and she took my picture. I had on my Boy Scout uniform. They wouldn't let me be a boy scout. But you can hardly tell the difference in the uniform. They call it a play suit! She said, "Supper isn't ready, but it will be in a little while. Come home pretty quick."

I don't have any flowers. But I go home anyway. That's all I remember. Never could spell too well.

Ida: I think it was because I couldn't see the blackboard. I'd just gotten my glasses. After that I did better. I studied real hard and I did better. I couldn't see the blackboard before and the teacher wrote the words on the blackboard, so I never knew what they were.

Dr. S.: O.K. You're doing fine...let yourself relax deeply, now knowing that you will be able to go back to the birth experience, and you may recall impressions and be able to talk and describe the impressions, even though you may not have been able to talk at that time. Let yourself relax deeply.

(Long pause)

"Moeun," a Gray. Self sketch via "D."

Cranial index extremely large.

Eyes full of compassion and understanding. Eyeglasses are built into space suit and are formed to fit head contour. Glasses seem to enlarge eyes, suggesting a hypnotic effect.

More pronounced joint bones than in human bodies, but softened by the space suit.

Completely covered by a two-piece grey metallic spacesuit, joined at the waist by a "breather belt" that "welds" the pieces together. Suit is used more as a decontamination unit on Earth than as a space suit.

Very long fingers, possibly with four joints rather than three like ours, and no thumbs.

Ida: Big room. Wide boards. Little rugs. Big bed. I am not in bed. I'm up there. High. I asked to come here. It is my duty. I must be born here. Not as the babies are born, but into the understanding and consciousness of the one who is dead. I will be her mind, her consciousness, her feelings. *No* one will ever know that I was not born. The body I occupy was born, but that was not I. They must revive that body to breathe before I can enter. I wish they would hurry up. It will be too late. Now. Now is the time. I must forget all that went before. I must forget who I am. I must not remember until it is time to remember, when all the others will be called upon to know, for they are many. It is so long waiting. No, not now. This is not the time. I must wait. The time will come for all. Not, now. (Then louder, with strong emotion.) Not now! (Pause, then comes out of hypnosis.)

Ida: Hi!

Dr. S.: Hi! How are you doing?

Ida: I'm not sure. I'm not sure.

Dr. S.: Experiencing some difficult feelings there?

Ida: No. Now that I'm awake. I'm not sure.

Dr. S.: Um, I see. I was wondering when you said, not now—whether you were talking about the way you felt in this situation or how you felt at the time of the experience?

Ida: Now is not the time to know...I feel like I'm making it all up.

Dr. S.: (Laughs)

Ida: I do. I really do. But I'm not.

Dr. S.: That's right.

Ida: I don't know that much.

Dr. S.: The feeling you had was like an out-of-body experience and looking down?

Ida: Waiting. Just waiting. Waiting somewhere. Somewhere in the room, waiting.

Dr. S.: To go into the body. Then the feeling was that you had a special mission or purpose or task?

Ida: Duty. Duty is not a mission. There was a choice. I could come here or stay. The other person chose first to stay and work from that side. I suppose I came here to work from this side...guess we gotta get together some of these days. Bridge.

Dr. S: A bridge. Between that life and that world and this world and this life?

Ida: To interpret. That is my duty—to interpret. I don't know what.

End of first session.

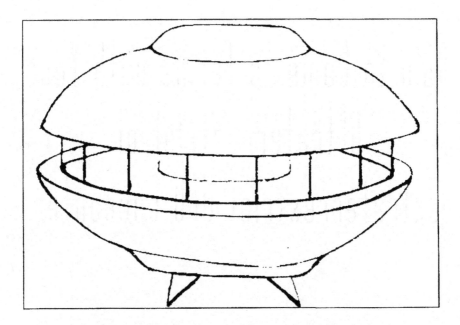

Extraterrestrial craft open for observation.

Subsequently I learned that the two men who spoke to me when I was seven were the same two who took me aboard the UFO in 1940. They were my communicators, Amorto and Jamie. Hweig was the injured one. He had fallen on some rocks when he tried to leave the UFO to come meet me. "The other person" mentioned above is The Hidden One!

Part II

How to Come to Terms with Your Ultraterrestrial or Extraterrestrial UFO Encounter

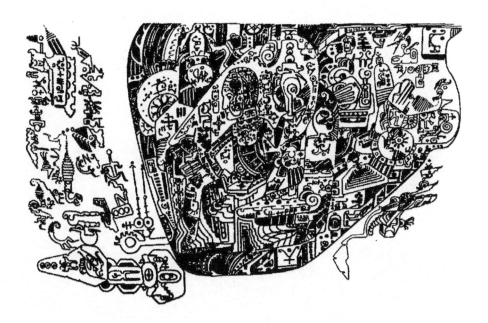

This shows a personage trying to classify and organize his experiences even as you and I.

About the Artist

Julie Wilkinson is a contactee who has been taught to draw in this fascinating manner. She had no art experience before she started these drawings [in Part II]. "I just hold the pen over the paper," says Julie, "and let my hand go. At first the drawings were quite primitive, but they continue to become more and more complex.

Julie does not know what the pictures and the symbols represent nor why she is being made to draw them.

I had not heard of Julie, nor she of me, until she was told I like to decipher symbols. Then she sent me a box of about 400 drawings, all 14" x 17" and very impressive in their original size.

She could not have not drawn better illustrations for this book if she had known all about it!

Ida M. Kannenberg

Preface

Generalized Viewpoint

The reason science has had such a hard task pulling any sense out of the UFO mystery is that science is so compartmentalized. We have a behavioral scientist over here, a parapsychologist over there, and a hard fact nuts-and-bolts man some other where. As long as they sit miles apart, each trying to pull his own thread from the mystery, they are not going to unravel anything except each other's patience.

They must meet on common ground and all agree on a common basis of reference. Each of them has something as important and valuable and necessary to contribute as the others.

Maybe if we sat all three in the middle of the floor and cracked their heads together, as my mother used to do when my brother and I quarreled over a puzzle, they would all commiserate with one another and become friends. (We always did—at least for a time!)

It will take all three working from a common workbox, the hard-fact man, the behaviorist, the psychic explorer. The sooner they get that common workbox arranged, the sooner the seams of the mystery will begin to unravel.

In the meantime we have to work with what we have. And what we have of the UFO mystery so far, thanks to the painstaking efforts of qualified investigators, are two outstanding facts:

1.   UFO experiences are real.

2.   The psychological impact on the contactees follows a definite pattern.

With that much known for sure (I guess you could call these our constants), we can come to at least some partial conclusions, if not total answers. Even that much will help in reassuring the truly suffering contactees that:

1.   They are not alone.

2.   They are not crazy.

You have no idea how comforting, stabilizing and necessary those assurances are unless you have been there.

And pardner, I was there!

In this writing I have tried to interweave two threads of purpose:

1. To discover how the UFO event related to the process of initiation.

2. To discover by what means the event was presented.

Of course the process of initiation does not clear up the total explanation of the UFO mystery, but it does serve to clarify some of the issues, and to reassure contactees that there is a valuable reason for the ordeals they have undergone.

Was the experience

1. a physical fact?

2. a dream?

3. a mind vision?

4. an induced hallucination?

5. an illusion?

6. an out-of-body experience?

7. mind travel?

8. mental telepathy?

9. whispered voices?

10. unheard compulsions?

All of these things are possible, and all of them are induced by those UFO characters. There are, no doubt, other possibilities as well, but I write only what I have had some experience with, or been given some knowledge about. I am not just guessing.

I'm crazy? Fine! Have your own opinion, but doesn't it seem a useful and practical kind of crazy? It serves a purpose and helps those in distress. And it is provable, or at least supportable, by the facts patiently garnered by all those competent investigators. Do a little homework before your final judgment. I have been doing mine in a formal sense for 24 years and in an informal one for a lifetime.

The investigator must regard the contactee's own interpretation of his encounter as the most vital clue he has to work with. Add to this his understanding of the individual contactee and a pattern of reference devised from the study of many encounters, and he can begin to suspect, with some validity, some of the hidden factors behind it all.

An investigator works from five necessities:

1.   A contactee whose integrity is unquestionable.

2.   An investigative analysis of the contactee's cultural background.

3.   An in-depth analysis of the contactee's psychological background.

4.   Knowledge of the psychological impact of the experience on the contactee.

5.   A pattern of reference based on the analysis of many encounters.

Such a pattern is attempted here, a pattern based on the process of initiation. This pattern is not chosen arbitrarily from a personal viewpoint, it is the pattern the course of many contactee experiences impose upon us.

Dr. Carl G. Jung believed the process that he called individuation, the ultimate goal in life, is a definite initiatory process, ordeals and all. In this UFO reference I believe the initiation pattern was deliberately planned for each individual, and relentlessly accelerated toward fulfillment.

We have scientists who have become obsessed with the value of statistics and of other rigid concepts that may not be as close to gospel as they would like to believe.

"If you can't count it, it doesn't exist. If you can't replicate it, it's a hoax. If you can't pickle it in a bottle or label it on a shelf, it is useless, discard it."

Thank heavens there are some daring enough, smart enough, and courageous enough to begin to question other realities. Hopefully their answers will not be swept under the rug by the scornful majority.

Perhaps, we as the general public have been too eager to create a myth of scientific infallibility. "Science has all the answers."

Don't blame the scientists for foisting this upon us. We did it to ourselves.

Our fairy godmothers deserted us, and we had to have somebody to lean on. We depend on everyone except ourselves and blame them when they fail, not realizing that it is we who have failed ourselves.

If we want to know the answers to the UFO mystery, there will have to be some changes. The scientific stance will have to bend in new directions and learn to accommodate new kinds of evidence. If it does not, we will abandon our myth and undertake the gentle art of inquisitiveness ourselves. In this case the sacred domain of science will suffer a rupture of faith that can never be repaired, and scientists will come to be looked upon as data technicians and mechanics.

The shift in the scientific viewpoint is excruciatingly slow and long overdue. A few courageous pioneers have already made the leap, but quietly and not too calmly wait in great frustration to be recognized and joined by others, who, from little fault of their own, are pressured by life's exigencies into the ponderous snail's pace of extreme caution. Many hearts have made the leap, but hands are cuffed and legs ironed by the opinions and demands of those they must respect.

Psychic phenomena are real. More than that, they are a natural part of man's heritage. We have forgotten. The "SBs" are old pros using them to bewilder and befuddle us in a thousand different ways. We will never find out what they are up to by counting portholes and fingers and trips to Venus or Mars or Clarion.

By SBs we can mean two things: Superior Beings or Sons-of-Bs, depending on our latest experience. I use Superior to mean superior in knowledge, and they are certainly that! To some it might mean Space Brothers, but we must use this warily, it is not altogether certain this includes them all. Or any.

Since this is not meant to be a scientific treatise, but a means of helping other contactees to interpret their own experiences, I will not go into the use of the science of psychic phenomena at this time. And psychic phenomena are a science. They're not magic and not supernatural. They don't originate in the spiritual realm or by divine decree. So I have been informed. To quote my informant (one of those SBs) directly:

"It truly seems strange that we must start in the very primer of the subject, and even there you do not know your ABCs. We are quite consternated and a little anguished to learn how little the world knows, or believes, or accepts manifestations of psychic being, even when it is part of themselves. We flounder in a morass of confusion where to start to reveal these matters, which are so basic to us it is like breathing or walking to you. We have forgotten how we go about it, and to try to put it into descriptive words makes us stumble and choke, just as you would if you tried to describe how you walk or breathe.

"To start with basics, we must reiterate again that psychic being is a part of your natural self, and psychic powers are many within you. They have been atrophied from lack of use and educated out when they appeared spontaneously.

"So long as the world refuses to believe in this basic text, so long will it go without powers it can use to make mankind and the earth a place of real harmony and happiness.

"In essence, the only thing holding men back from reclaiming the powers and elevations they once knew is the willingness to believe, at least to believe long enough to learn. Then, and only then, can they know.

"Men, in early ages, found their psychic powers just as they discovered their powers of sight and hearing. They were there, organs in use and used wisely, for unwise use created disease and disaster, just as unwise use of your eyes creates blindness. The powers were natural and free to all who were born human.

"The use of the powers was learned at the mother's knee, just as the ABCs are generally learned in your world today. When the small child had grown in understanding and stature, the father usually took over the teaching. Later, after culture progressed to such a point, the teacher or tutor took over. Later came the shaman or witch doctor. And that is where the trouble and the decline began. When the teaching was held in the hands of a favored few, they found it was power over the common man and his world, and they never gave the power back. It became taboo for the common person to use some of the greatest of the powers; only the shaman or spiritual leader could do so. And the powers are not spiritual, but psychic! They should always have been kept in the hands of the ordinary everyday persons, each developing according to his inherent capacities and limitations, and according to his own interests and ambitions. They are a natural part and power of Man!

"Hypnosis, its full understanding and use, telepathy, and all the other psychic powers must be studied anew and a way found to reunite man with his rightful heritage, at the same time giving no man power over his neighbor.

"Some of the most heathen and backward people have kept alive their knowledge and use of psychic powers, while the enlightened and scientific people have let it die."

I could quote many hundreds of words on this subject, but that is not the point of this writing. We will save that for a later time.

Why do we so steadfastly refuse to listen to what they are telling us? Because it sounds weird, strange and impossible, and we fear the consequences of accepting the untried and unproven? How can we try to prove it if we won't listen?

We don't have a key? Is there a key? Indeed, yes!

They are not showing us facts: they are showing us ideas they want us to think about, and they are doing so through various psychic processes for the most part. These processes express the ideas in *symbols* that the SBs believe will speak to us, for they have been chosen from our own cultures. If we interpret the contactee experience on that basis, they will indeed speak to us.

That is the key: psychic phenomena are used to present symbols to get across ideas that they want us to think about. Things seen that are not actual cultural symbols are still representative of ideas they want us to recognize and study.

The formula: *ideas + symbols = think*!

Rule Number 1: If you can't tell tit from tat, don't tot!

I have known investigators (rather amateur ones to be sure) who strove mightily to get a higher tally of something like portholes in their portfolio than their colleagues, or to categorize their data in the most minute detail, an exercise in futility! If they can't tell which is fact and which is illusion, what good is a tally?

Caution: don't try to pattern a better aircraft on an illusion. Someone may have invented that ultra-porthole just for pretty. It may be durable for five minutes. Unless, of course, the contactee is a design engineer for aircraft, then he may have been given a valid inspiration for practical use, but not if he was a bartender out for a day of fishing. No offense to bartenders! Contactees are put through long and rigorous training to make sure that the material they are given can be and will be used. A bartender would have little use for a better porthole.

Does it really matter all that much who those SBs really are and where they are from? Only fear pushes that need to know into our minds. Why should they even want to tell us the truth about themselves when we have paid so little attention to the valuable information they have already given us? We need to think about the ideas behind the symbols that they have given.

As for purpose—the psychological impact on the contactee is all the purpose we can discover at this time. Let us utilize this information, then maybe we will get some more.

What does it matter how many fingers the occupant had, or how many portholes were in the craft? How would we possibly make any use of that knowledge? (But the idea of four fingers points back to the gods of several very ancient civilizations. Is there a connection with SBs?) What does matter is what the contactees did about their experiences.

- Have they learned anything useful about themselves?
- Have they done anything beneficial for humankind?
- Have they learned a new respect for the laws and things of nature?

That is the importance of the UFO event as far as we are concerned.

As far as the SBs are concerned, how can we know? Perhaps the tasks that they undertake with us are part of *their initiatory process!*

They are much too clever to give away purposes or reasons until they are ready to do so, and they will never be ready if we do not make use of what they have already so generously given us.

UFO investigators have been dutifully counting such things as:

How many times were form chairs reported?

metal floors?

square windows?

cylinders? and, of course,

portholes?

If we do not know how many encounters were actual physical events, how many induced hallucinations, inspired dreams, out-of-body experiences or projected images, can we use the counting of statistics for any purpose?

But, if we start counting psychological facts, such as:

- How many contactees thought they met Jesus?
- How many thought they visited a beautiful and peaceful world?
- How many thought they were given a task that was vital to the survival of mankind?

Now we can tally up such totals and have a revelation of the extent and limitations of the human mind and the quality of the human condition. We have discovered facts that can be utilized by psychologists, sociologists, or even environmentalists, politicians and propagandists. Now the UFO experience becomes pertinent to our daily lives as it was meant to be.

It is necessary of course that, as investigators, we collect some static background material, but if that is all we collect, then we are as static as our material. Static patterns and static investigators will stand like Lot's wife, frozen in time, forever looking backward.

To be truly useful, a pattern must not only accept everything whether agreeable to one's own premise or not, but be flexible and accepting when additional knowledge and conditions necessitate.

The only criterion that should determine if an encounter is to be examined and included is the integrity of the contactee. Is he patently and honestly telling exactly what he perceived, thought and felt, as well as any human being can report such an experience?

It scarcely matters if the occupant really had four fingers or five, as long as the contactee honestly and fervently thought he saw four. Four becomes the psychological fact, and psychological facts are the best we can ever hope to discern and count in any comprehensive research of the UFO encounter.

We must consider every encounter a precious and unique opportunity to learn something, whether that something coincides with our prior beliefs and intentions or not.

In pursuing the psychological fact, we are not only studying the psychological states as evidenced by the contactees, we are exploring the outer limits of human consciousness.

As human beings:
- How far are we able to perceive?
- How far are we able to believe?
- How far are we willing to discover ourselves?

And another question of the UFO mystery becomes: *Who are we?*

This book is an attempt to help contactees compare their own experiences with others and to see that they are not being deliberately abused, but that there is a meaning and a purpose in it all. They are urged to compare their own condition relative to the pattern given, and to help themselves find a way into their future. Few investigators are prepared at present to do this: they do not have the keys.

The answers here are tentative, but they will have to do until better ones come along. They do help, being evolved from the experience and study, and presented with the care and concern of the writer, with considerable input from those who devised the experiences, the SBs themselves. They should know what they are doing and why and how.

If this were a court of law, I would not ask such leading questions, but how can a contactee get over the shock and jolt of his strange and bizarre experience without some guidance in evaluating the things seen and done? He can only know how to report what happened when he has some idea of what is important to report, perhaps even why it is important. Fear of sounding silly, being ridiculed, thought crazy or accused of lying may hold back some very essential details that he deems of no value.

Did the lights dim down and go out, then flare up again when they were taken into the round room on the craft? An item of no consequence, they won't bother to mention it? Oh, but it was! It was a symbol itself, or actually a signal, that the old life was to die—the dimming down and going out of the light—and a new life was to begin—the flaring up of the light. Almost everything those SBs do should be interpreted on the basis of symbolism.

I believe this must have something to do with the fact that, as they have said innumerable times, they communicate with each other through pictorial telepathy. They are accustomed to getting their ideas across to each other through pictures, and so they plan ideas, expressed through symbols, both static and in action, to communicate with us. It is just simpler than trying out a multitude of languages, or explaining ideas in a dictatorial fashion.

They are not infallible! Even they have confessed that. They did not realize our word symbology had evolved so far from its pictorial origins that we had forgotten and would be hard put to understand this key.

Symbols in action, all those little staged presentations, are not to be taken as factual at all, but as the ideas they represent. They chose their symbology from our own past, self-assured that we would understand, as they were symbols from our own legends, myths, religions and ancient cultures. To understand them, we have to train ourselves to think in pictorial ideas and to interpret them from our own cultural past. Visualization of ideas takes a terrific amount of concentration and practice to learn, a lot of self-training.

Dear Contactee:

All those little pictures that come up in your mind and keep you from going to sleep are for the purpose of training you to think visually. It takes long practice. Discovering the meaning and purpose will save a lot of floundering, time and wear and tear on the nervous system. Work with it, not against it. Try to see the ideas that the mind visions express.

If you have ever tried to train yourself in writing fiction, you will have a good head start, for current fiction, written with one eye on sale to the movies or TV, involves a lot of visualization. Perhaps that is why in the past many of you have spent a great deal of time learning to write fiction, plays or screen scripts. All has been planned long ahead. No contact is accidental. Your whole life has meaning and purpose to specific ends.

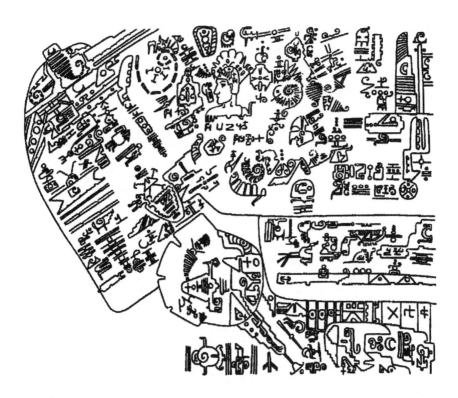

In this section I warn contactees about allowing themselves to be picked to pieces by amateur investigators and their questionnaires. Psychologically it is very difficult to put oneself back together again and function thereafter without stress. The poor fellow shown here has been picked completely to pieces and left to fend for himself, all alone.

Foreword

Part II

"No one wants to help me. They won't listen, or they only listen to jeer. They tell me I am crazy. I am all alone and scared."

How many hundreds of contactees throughout the world hear their own voices echoed in these words?

I, too, have been to the lair where waited the silvery ship. I have known the agonies of doubt and confusion and the terrible fear of going insane, and I have cringed under words of ridicule and rejection. I have seen the side winks and twisted smiles.

After many years, I have come to a peaceable co-existence with the UFO mysteries. My resolutions may not solve everything, but they help me to accept my participation with less fear and more grace. Perhaps they can help others.

That is the reason for, and purpose of, this book. By following the text and answering the questions with details of your own experiences, you can find enough of a tenable answer to your own situation that the agonies of tension and insecurity are greatly alleviated.

That is the whole purpose of this book—to assure you that you are not alone in your experience, that your observations are not the result of pathological or mental aberrations no matter how bizarre, fantastic, ludicrous or impossible they may seem. Somewhere in the event there is a dimension of reality, and even, perhaps, a purpose.

If we wait for total answers to solve the total mysteries, nothing will ever be done to alleviate the fear or distress of the contactees. Such a writing as this, partial though it may be, is needed *now*. It won't be needed at all when those total answers are in. Personally I doubt they ever will be!

You, a contactee, have not merely had a sighting, an observation, or an encounter. You have participated in an event that will color and shape the rest of your life.

My purpose is to tell what the factors of that event mean in your past and future life. That is what I do know about, from personal experience, from much long and concentrated study of many UFO experiences, and with much input from those SBs themselves. (See Preface.)

My contacts in the last twelve years have been mostly through mental telepathy, before that—through hell! It is sometimes difficult to accept those SBs as the benign friends they would make themselves out to be. The trials and tribulations they put us through hardly seem the acts of loving friends.

Even here, there is a caring purpose—cleansing our tough minds and tender psyches in a way and to a degree we never would undertake by ourselves, putting us through the fire of -*initiation?*

Many times I have said, "But this is like an initiation." The question was, into what? Whatever, and presently we shall consider this in more detail; it served the purpose of clarifying and strengthening of the self mentally and psychologically. There is much more in the UFO event than initiation, but the process of initiation is there, and should be recognized and evaluated.

I write with the assumption that if a contactee can get any kind of a handle on any part of his experience he will be vastly relieved, and perhaps his life can go forward with less hassle.

The chapter questions will ask, in essence:

- What happened to you?
- What did you do in reaction or response to it?
- How did you feel?
- What did you think?
- Has the event in any way affected your life, a change of habits, activities, aims or purposes?

About half of the UFO events are tests having to do with character clarification and development, which are also purposes behind the initiatory process.

About three-eighths have to do directly with the rituals and symbols of initiation. The remaining one-eighth is meant to be general information not necessarily related to the initiatory process. This ratio is not exact, of course, but any kind of a proportionate division will help us to identify the several purposes in the event.

The test issues have to do directly with character development. They make us think, analyze, evaluate, weigh, judge and choose our next course of action.

The initiatory scenes are to make us realize, understand, accept and perhaps to put us a little (or a lot) in awe or to strengthen our curiosity. This is where the SBs are inclined to overdo things and scare the hell out of us. The information is meant as comforting, consoling or confirming of something we have already decided, and are mainly to make us stop our fuss.

They care, believe me they do, but they are never inclined to be lenient. You run the course or else become a drop-out. Only they decide that, not you.

When you have completed your questions as well as you can, you may do with them whatever you like. Keep them entirely to yourself to mull over and add to if future discoveries are made, to revise as future events dictate or to send a photocopy to some investigator, investigative group, scientist or to Wild Flower Press for confidential archiving. But by all means keep the original intact. You may want to find a friend or friendly group with allied interests to discuss each other's situations.

Now I must impose some private grievances. The recital may save you from much disappointment and a little anger. Beware of any interviewer who calls on the phone and asks many questions. You don't know really who he or she represents or how he or she intends to use your answers. It could mean storing up embarrassment or trouble for yourself.

If you answer a lengthy questionnaire when there has been no promise of an evaluation or even answer, you will feel exploited and angry. Rightfully so. Be certain that you know how your information will be used and that you will receive the consideration of a personal reply and some kind of assessment.

Beware of breaking yourself up into many tiny fragments required by questionnaires and sending them off into oblivion. Psychologically it is most difficult to piece yourself back together again and function smoothly thereafter. You will feel that parts of you are missing or have gone astray, into what adventure you know not. Pieces and questions keep rising up in your mind to haunt you, often hurtfully.

Our cautions summarized:

- Know for certain whom you are talking or writing to, more than just a name.
- Know for certain what he or she intends to do with all those bits and pieces of you.

- Know that you will receive the consideration of a thoughtful and caring reply. They *owe* you that much for you tearing yourself to bits for *their* investigation.

There are so many amateur investigators who do not know the rules and ethics. One man phoned me, told me he was "researching" and began a barrage of questions. For a few minutes I replied amiably, then I realized he could not possibly be writing down the answers—his questions were too rapid.

"Are you tape recording this?"

"Well, uh, yeah."

I answered about three more questions, found I was getting angry, excused myself and hung up. If he had asked permission to record in the beginning I would have said, "Fine," and I would have turned on my own recorder so that I, too, would have evidence later of what was really said. I am most willing to cooperate, but not with the devious. It meant instant distrust.

Another caution: If you have written material dictated or drawings inspired by a mental contact and you want to share this with others, be certain that you retain in writing all copyrights. You could find your best material copyrighted by someone else and lost thereafter to your own use. There are fine, well-trained, experienced, ethical investigators and scientists you can depend on.

Be helpful and willing to cooperate with all legitimate and responsive investigators. It is only by analysis and comparison of all available material that the larger answers can be found. But don't let yourself be ravaged and exploited by the thoughtless and uncaring.

It is necessary to write out your answers in some kind of notebook so that you may check back as you proceed and see where the pattern of initiation begins to emerge. Be as detailed as possible, but don't guess, assume or manufacture. If there is no answer, response or memory for a question at the moment, go on to the next. Other bits will pop up as you continue. Go back at once and fill them in before you forget again. Don't linger so long on one question that your imagination begins to fantasize in spite of your best intentions.

A fantasy story will become a bugaboo in your future. You may create a fantasy you cannot control.

Warning: By a strange psychological process such fantasies can begin to serve as realities. You cannot always anticipate the total consequences of unbridled invention.

Since you are doing this exercise for your own benefit, it behooves you to be as desperately accurate as you can. Otherwise there is no point in your doing it. Write fiction instead. Be very positive of the accuracy of all your statements. Later, if you want to contact a professional investigator or scientist, you will have well thought-out notes to photocopy.

The questions will call to mind many bits of information lying just under the surface of consciousness. They need only a touch of recognition to spring from the subconscious into recall. Some remembered bits you pass over as inconsequential. The text questions will make apparent that every tiny bit is of the utmost importance. The color of a wall is as important as the appearance of the beings who confront you. Believe it!

To quote Mircea Eliade, *Rites and Symbols of Initiation:* "The depth psychologist has taught us that a symbol delivers its message and fulfills its function even when its meaning escapes the conscious mind."

And symbols are precisely what the UFO experience is giving us. Some are cultural, some literary, some historical and some mythological, which is a combination of literature, culture, history, written or oral.

If you have dreams that seem to be trying to tell you something, or dreams so vivid that you would stake your life that they were real, or even momentary visions "in the mind's eye" with a strong and lasting impression, and you cannot identify what is causing this disturbance, it might be well to see a hypnotist who is hep to the UFO phenomena.

If hypnosis does not bring complete and satisfactory relief/recall, be content to wait a little. When the time is right there will be total recall, as well as returning memory for many other things, some of which you will wish you could forget!

You have been timed to remember, but if these bits of recall cause worry, worry, worry, perhaps it is intended for you to start a probe to help the process. No one is controlling your mind. A seed has been planted, and you must help it to germinate.

Questions

1. Date
2. Full name
3. Address
4. Phone number
5. Age
6. Work or Business
7. Formal years of education
8. Special training
9. Persons living in home and relationship
10. Are you active in politics? (yes or no)
11. Are you church affiliated? (yes or no)
12. Was your UFO experience
    a. a sighting only?
    b. observation of landed craft/occupants?
    c. confrontation with occupants?
    d. Were you taken into a craft or other place?
    e. Was there any communication between you and the occupants? Was this verbal or mental? Relate briefly.
    f. Was the experience a one-time thing or has it been ongoing, and in what manner? Relate briefly for now, more later.
13. Do you consider yourself psychic and/or have you had what seemed to be psychic experiences? Relate briefly.
14. Were your parents or other close members of your family considered psychic?
15. What time of day or night did your first UFO experience occur?
16. Where were you and what were you doing at the time of your first UFO experience?
17. Have you reached any conclusions about the meaning of this (or these) experience(s) in your life?

You will have the opportunity to tell more in future chapters.

In this picture we see the highly stylized serpent that represents secular knowledge. The man's face is black, but not his hands. Black indicates something unknown, perhaps he does not really "Know himself." He is reaching toward the right, hand cupped, asking for knowledge of an opposite kind. See the square spiral below his arm. A spiral always indicates an ascension from a lower to a higher. It is the symbol of initiation. He is asking for initiation into spiritual knowledge.

CHAPTER ONE

The Process of Initiation

So you are a contactee? I can tell you two things about yourself right now—your general character traits, and whether or not you will have or have had extensive UFO encounters or mental contacts:

- You are open minded, willing to consider anything as long as it is moral and decent.
- You are curious, have to investigate and figure out things.
- You are generous, to a fault maybe.
- You are appalled at the condition of the world and spend much time thinking about problems of war, poverty, hunger, disease, injustice and crime.
- You are courageous, maybe a little shy or retiring in some situations, but when real danger or disaster strikes, you are up to it.
- You are enduring, even stubborn. You will suffer a long time in an almost unbearable situation as long as you believe there is some good in doing so.
- You are loving and kind beyond the average.

If you can affirm that this outline of character is mostly true, you are in for a long siege with UFO experiences. You have been chosen for the full course of initiation.

Into what? The SBs have explained it to me thus: "Participation in a fellowship of acutely trained persons dedicated to the aims of helping peace and justice return to this world.

"This fellowship is composed of many, many kinds of personalities and persons, some within your world, some from many worlds away, for what concerns one of God's creatures concerns all. An infinitude of souls are collaborating in this endeavor, and from many worlds."

I was given the following plan in 1980 during the First Rocky Mountain UFO conference at the University of Wyoming in Laramie.

The Plan is the rejuvenation of Earth and its inhabitants.

A.   Rejuvenation through collaboration of UFO people with Earth's inhabitants.
    1.   Teaching, leading into new discoveries.
    2.   Drawing out of potentials and developing of latent abilities.
    3.   Organizing and extending knowledge.
    4.   Modifying present social structures.
    5.   Resolving current conflicts and threatening dangers of
        all categories.
B.   Rejuvenation through application of special knowledge and abilities of the UFO people.
    1.   Technological.
    2.   Scientific and medical.
    3.   Psychical.
C.   Rejuvenation through cultural exchange
    1.   Language.
    2.   Inter-communication of ideas.
    3.   Friendship and marriage.
    4.   Art and literary inspiration.
D.   Rejuvenation of people through rebirth of non-materialistic values.
    1.   Spirit of helpfulness.
    2.   Desire to be useful.
    3.   Reconstructed work ethic.
    4   Attitude of cheerfulness.
    5.   Cooperation and sharing.
E.   Rejuvenation of Earth
    1.   Physical
        a.   Land, cooperate with natural forces.
        b.   Forests, replenish and use wisely.

    c.   Water supplies, find substitutes for and new sources.

    d.   Plants.

  e.   All natural resources, value and replace.

  f.   To improve upon nature, and help her along with some of her destroyed or hindered plans.

2.   Sources of energy

  a.   To rebuild areas that have been depleted of deposits—oil, gas, coal, *etc.*

  b.   Find easier, less expensive sources of energy.

  c.   Find new ways to accomplish things that do not require such extensive uses of energy.

3.   Animal life

  a.   Restore dwindling species.

  b.   Breed healthier animals.

  c.   Control better living conditions for animals.

F.   Infiltration: (By various processes: telepathy enhanced by technological devices)

Regarding point F, no government can stop this kind of mental invasion by passing laws against it. It must be recognized that it exists. We must discover how it exists and above all, why it exists.

The above outline has been somewhat simplified from the original but states explicitly what the UFO people want us to believe they are here for. This may not be the whole story, but for the present it is what we have to work with. This writing, offered as a way to understand at least part of the UFO event, and by so much appease the anxiety and fears, hopes to find a little understanding among so much mystery.

At the end of this chapter I will give two incidents of the way in which the SBs work, but for now I am anxious to get on to an exposition of the pattern of initiation itself. This is not an analysis of the total UFO event as an initiation. It is meant to find the formula of initiation among the many questions and mysteries of the event.

A sense of belonging, direction, or rightness is some of the rewards of the initiate. It assures self of its worth and answers some of the questions the self constantly asks the self, "Who am I? What am I doing here? Where am I going?" It gives peace and stability at the center of self and promotes self-assurance above all.

I have simplified the elements and background of initiation down to the nub, maybe a little too much. More will be added as we progress through the chapters.

All initiation involves:

- Isolation or separation from others.
- Being led or sent, sooner or later, into a circular place or round enclosure.
- Observation of certain things meant as symbols.
- The assignment of tutors or mentors.
- The assignment of disciplines and ordeals.
- The spending of much time learning traditions and spiritual purposes of the community or society.
- The acceptance of tasks with a sense of climbing or ascension and the undertaking of journeys or quests.
- Revelations or visions at the apex of climbing or peak of ascension.
- Attainment of powers or abilities.
- Acceptance into a "higher order" or a place of elevated or greater responsibility.

All initiations follow the same basic pattern from the most primitive to the most sophisticated. (Primitive does not necessarily mean basic.)

Perhaps one of the richest and most profound uses of initiation today is that found in the ordination of priests or ministers. This sort of initiation begins with declaration of intent and separation for years of study. Vows are made, teachers are given, disciplines, tasks and ordeals are undertaken, and finally a total commitment is made to a way of life. This is what you, as a contactee, are undergoing. You say you did not make a declaration of intent? Think! Remember!

Sometime in your life, I do not have to ask, I know you did, you said, or thought, or prayed fervently and sincerely that you wished that you could do something to benefit your fellow man, to help alleviate the pain, suffering and hunger in the world. Oh yes, you did, and probably more than once.

Every contactee has this in common in their past pre-event life. They declared their intent and they meant it in a most unselfish, nonegoistic way and to a degree that was a prayer and a commitment.

You, yourself, by that declaration, chose to be a contactee. Of course you knew nothing about UFOs, but those SBs heard you. And responded.

Not all who make such declarations become contactees. Some become doctors, scientists, medical researchers or garbage collectors. They have already found their answer to their prayer.

But what if you are still dissatisfied with your life? You fret that the need to make a living or to care for others has veered you away from your desired course? You have been privately fussing and stewing to yourself, knowing that the trolley has gone off the track but not knowing how to get it back on again.

You are now ripe for your UFO experience. If you are lucky, and durable, and open minded enough to learn, the experience will come. "Don't call us we'll call you."

What happens after that first event is a process of getting acquainted, learning and training, an initiation period that can be as rugged as the Himalayas.

More than one such initiate has wound up in a hospital.

That is the sort of thing this writing is trying to avert. We do not have to submit to such extremes. I believe that more writing such as this is begging to be done. No doubt there are thousands who can add to my knowledge. I endorse their efforts heartily. Only, let's get on with it! There are a lot of suffering people out there!

As an example of a declaration of intent, I will impose my first declaration that I can remember. It was renewed many times thereafter.

When I was about seven years old I went with my Dad to his lodge meeting. (I guess for some reason I was superfluous at home). I was told to make myself invisible and pretend I wasn't there, as I wasn't supposed to be.

On the wall was a very large framed motto in beautiful, old-fashioned letters. I asked Dad what it was and he said it was the creed of that particular lodge and that a creed was something men lived by. While he went about his lodge business I sat behind a potted palm and memorized the words:

"I expect to pass through this life but once, therefore if there is any good I may do my fellow man or any kindness I may show, let me not defer nor neglect it, for I shall not pass this way again." (Attributed to one Stephen Millet, 1773-1855.)

I thought that a very fine thing to say and do, and I decided I would make that my creed too, never realizing that this was an open invitation to those SBs to come and get me.

It was and they came.

Some months later I was intercepted at play by two men. Later I remembered them talking to me, but I did not consciously recall what they had told me "in my head" until I was hypnotized many years later.

"Work harder at your spelling," the older man had said. "Learn to write well. Try to make nice sentences. Someday when you are much older you will write about wonderful things."

Well, I am much older by more than ten times, and I guess writing about wonderful things is exactly what I am doing. My subconscious understood and remembered all those years, though I consciously did not. All those years I obeyed without knowing it. That is the way those SBs work!

In the years of telepathic contact with the SBs I have run through every known emotion to them—aversion, disgust, anger, fear, and above all, skepticism. I frequently referred to them as liars, not understanding how their pieces of information fit together. I could see no fit, but I realize it was because I have too few pieces of the puzzle. After a hypnosis session with Dr. R. Leo Sprinkle, my skepticism abated a trifle so that I was no longer kicking and squealing at every idea they tried to impart.

The events they put us through are meant to develop us through experience, the only way to true actual development. Each of us is taught that which is uniquely "our thing." When enough contactees come out of the closet with their own stories, some of which they do not remember yet, because they are timed to remember, then we will see corroborations, coincidences and an overall pattern that will indeed "make sense." It will, hopefully, become believable and understandable. We will see that we are not ruthlessly invaded; we are extended in knowledge and experience.

This is all very well for explaining why they do what they do. But how is it all done? It just doesn't seem real! That, of course, is where all of this psychic flumdummery comes in.

Your experience was real. Don't let anybody talk you out of that reality. And it was for a purpose. The kind of reality may not be the ordinary humdrum reality of the material world. You may have hallucinated or had an illusion, but the experience was totally real and was induced on you by those SBs who know full well how to make it happen. That is why I call them SBs, both interpretations. The hallucination was not, I repeat, not a product of your own mind's origination. It was forced upon you by outside influence. To believe this does not mean you are paranoid. It means you are open- minded to realities that the general scientific research hasn't yet dared to explore.

These are the kinds of psychic experience:

Dreams

Mind visions

Induced hallucinations

Induced illusions

Out-of-body experiences

Mind travel

Mental telepathy

Whispered voices

Unheard compulsions

Levitation

There can also be projected images through holograms and lasers, but this is more technological. Technological devices may be used as an adjunct to the psychic process.

An experience that demonstrates both psychic event and symbolism is the story of Betty Andreasson. This was published by Raymond Fowler in his book, *The Andreasson Affair.* A detailed analysis of this story as an initiation was given by Amorto, one of the SBs, to Dr. R. Leo Sprinkle, who graciously allows us to use it here.

We will use only a skeleton outline of her experience for now. Later more details will be given. The events and symbols illustrate a perfect pattern of initiation, and indeed Betty herself said later, "It was like an initiation."

Betty's children and elders were frozen by hypnosis and remained in the home while Betty was apparently taken aboard a craft. Actually her body remained in its physical state in the home, and it was her out-of-body essence that was taken in semi-corporeal form on the excursion.

This is evidenced by the fact that Betty and her abductors were able to walk through the solid back door without opening it. Her condition and that of the little "men" were of a lessened density than the wood of the door. When she and her captors reached the craft it was necessary for them to open the door, as the craft was in the same semi-corporeal state that they were, i.e., all were of the same degree of density. The craft never left the backyard even in its semi-corporeal state. All her travels were illusions.

During any initiation there are two vows that are repeated at intervals, but in various ways, not always verbally. These two are to obey God and to work for the benefit of others. Betty repeated these vows by her reactions and also verbally.

Her main abductor was one of the little big-heads, or grays, we meet so often in UFO reports. He gave his name as "Quazgaa." Quazgaa asked Betty for "food burnt by fire," which he meant to symbolize knowledge learned by the struggles and ordeals of life. He was asking Betty to reveal the state of her spiritual condition. This was misunderstood, but she gave him a Bible.

Betty's examination began with a ritual bath, symbolic of spiritual cleansing, which is part of many, many initiations, as is our baptism. It was intended to offer her a new garment, symbolic of donning a new way of life, but Betty's distress was so acute that they allowed her to put on her own clothing again.

The physical examination was illusory. No needle or instrument was used, but she thought it was and her fear created pain. Passing the hands over her face erased the fear, and thus the pain was eased.

She was told that she was not completely filled with light, that something was missing. She took this to mean that they referred to her hysterectomy. Actually they meant that there were gaps in her understanding. Quazgaa told her, "You have not understood the word you have. You've misunderstood in some places."

The examination brought out the physical idea of procreation and regeneration, as the Phoenix would later bring out the idea of spiritual rebirth. Also the cleansing, the examination, and the discussion of being filled with light symbolized that she herself was to undergo a change, an awakening in the spiritual sense. Soul and spirit are not synonymous.

Throughout the event there was a slow and steady process from semi-corporeal reality into one of pure symbolism and toward pure illusion. Betty was seated in a form chair, and from here on everything was illusion. Her mind went traveling, and since her mind is the most real part of her, she experienced the events very, very realistically.

We now have poor Betty in three conditions of being; her physical self is still in the house, while her semi-corporeal self, derived from her psychic essence or soul-self, is seated in the form chair, and at the same time her mind self, or spirit-on-earth self, is prepared to go into the tunnel, where all is symbolism and illusion.

The whole "self is, of course, safely bonded by her mind, which is all one mind. Most earth persons can be capable of only one focus or awareness of mind at a time. A high adept or master can be aware of three or even five focuses all at once!

Betty thought she was covered with liquid and traveling, probably in space. This is precisely how space travel is done for earth people on occasion, but in this case it was pure illusion. During this time she was undergoing a process we call sleep learning. Her mind was being filled with a great deal of information that will come forth at various times in the future when it is needed.

Once they arrived, they entered a tunnel that appeared to her to be cut from stone, or like coal. This represents that it was a "natural" progress. Earth-born persons travel by natural progression through unenlightened ways, a tunnel. After many trials and ordeals, they come to the entrance to the final initiation. In Betty's case this was symbolized by a mirror. The glass shows self to self. Next she went through a death to the natural world, symbolized by the red area in which there was no vegetation or life. Then she passed through a membrane, regeneration, into a green area denoting new growth and life.

After observing many symbols, Betty came into the Radiance and was given an ordeal by fire. The Radiance represented the idea of God. She witnessed the burning and resurrection of the Phoenix, the symbol of rebirth. She thought she heard the "voice of God," an experience which is duplicated in rituals of many initiations.

It would take too long to interpret all the symbols here, so we will return to this again in Chapter Four. But we can see that Betty went through all the states of initiation, from the moment she was separated from her family, taken into the round enclosure of craft and put through various ordeals and situations pertinent to initiatory process.

Many times I have complained to SBs about their treatment. "Why don't you tell me what you are going to do?" and "Why can't you play fair?"

"We cannot tell you beforehand that you are to undergo certain experiences and what they will mean. If we did, you would color your responses and shape them to fit what you thought you ought to do and say.

"That would negate, wipe out, the purpose of the whole experience. Your reaction must be totally spontaneous and unconscious."

But if I asked afterward what the experience was supposed to mean,

"It means think. You are supposed to think!"

The SBs themselves have told me how and why they use manifestations of a psychic nature. These are many times augmented and enhanced by technological devices. I see no reason why we should not listen to the people who know, the perpetrators themselves. So I quote:

"Our manifestations are most carefully adapted to the individual, the suitability of occasion and understanding of the contactee, whom we have carefully studied over a long period of time and know very well indeed. No contact is accidental.

"Manifestations fall roughly into seven major categories with a multitude of sub-varieties. We can speak now of only the most significant ones:

Seven Forms of Manifestation

1.   "Manifestations of a semi-corporeal self. We manifest ourselves in what to all appearances is as physical and corporeal a condition as yourselves, but if you touched us with any material object, we simply would not be there. You could walk right through us, or we through you. We are then only semi- corporeal, visible and audibly so, but of a different corporeality than your own, not as dense, and of a substance of a much higher vibratory rate.

2.   "Manifestation of craft in the same degree of semi-corporeality. To all appearances it is there, but it can disappear in a second, and seemingly reappear instantaneously a great distance away.

3.   "Manifestation of events through auditory sounds or visual scenes. You would stake your life that you heard or saw something (like the visitor to Versailles) and in a deeper sense you did, but it is not there in the physical vibratory sense.

4.   "Manifestations of something being done to you physically. If you accept this without fear, there will be no adverse effect, not even pain. To struggle against it in fear creates pain and mental anguish

"It is easier to devise these illusory experiences than it is to send craft and persons from great distances away, or to engineer a 'real' event, and the results are absolutely the same! If the contactee went through the experience or only thought he went through the experience, the end result is the same. In certain instances then, illusion serves just as valid a purpose as actuality!

5.   "To obtain other ends, accomplish other purposes on other occasions, we must resort to actual physical events and appear in actual hardware craft, and in our actual corporeal physical beings. To interact physically with you, we must appear in our physical selves.

6.   "We can enter your world in our out-of-body state as you call it. We are then, of course, totally invisible, though we can take on semi-corporeality instantaneously if we wish. As psychic masters we can move in and out of these states at will and have complete control of our intent and actions.

7.   We can deliver our messages by several methods; what you call automatic writing, telepathic writing, in which the receiver hears the words as he writes them, he can hear an actual physical vibration as though someone were whispering in his ear, or he can receive a movement of meaning or words in his mind without physical vibration. It is almost as though one were talking to oneself! There are other ways and variations in which we get our meanings across, but this is sufficient for here.

"And another method of communication to our contactees is through sleep learning. While he is asleep things are being entered into his mind that he will not consciously remember when he wakes. It will emerge in a person's consciousness as a kind of inspiration, a sudden intuition or intuitive idea, a hunch, a brilliant resolution to a long standing problem."

How to tell whether you are receiving sleep learning:

1.   When you wake suddenly do you hear a sentence going on in your head that comes to an abrupt halt?

2.   Do you instantly forget what was said?

3.   Do you awake very tired sometimes, but in 15 minutes to half an hour you feel all fresh, inspired and ready to go?

4.   Do you ever receive at a moment of great distress or need a sudden brilliant thought that surprises you?

5.   Are you consistently aware that your thoughts seem directed or guided more than usual, or with great good luck?

6.   Do you have sudden strong thoughts that you need to do something, or have something, or know something, but can't quite grasp what it is, and then suddenly it just strikes you?

7.   Do you work all day and half the night on some vital problem and awake in the morning with the answer in your head?

8.   Do all of these inspirations, sudden thoughts or hunches have something to do with benefits for other people, one or more or many?

The last question is the conclusive one, and if your answer is yes to this one as well as to most of the others, then you undoubtedly have been prompted by UFO sleep learning.

How to tell if a sighted craft is an illusion:

1.   If photographed, did the object appear in the finished print? If not, the craft was an illusion, and semi-corporeal. If the object was printed, then it had to be a physical craft. Did you try to take pictures, and if so, with what result?

2.   Was the day sunny, cloudy or completely overcast? What was the color of the craft compared to the color of the sky? If there was very sharp contrast, the craft was physical. If there was very little contrast so that the appearance of the craft was hard to hold in the vision, then it was semi-corporeal. Illusionary craft absorb the color of the background.

3.   If observed nearing the surface of the earth, did the craft remain stable in motion, or did it see-saw from side to side? If it see-sawed in a slipping side-to-side motion, it was a real "nutz and boltz" craft. If it came down smoothly and steadily it was a hallucination. Physical craft must maneuver against certain energies on earth's surface to land or approach closely, therefore the side-to-side weaving of an actual physical craft.

4.   If observed already on land, were its landing legs extended beyond the circumference of the craft, or did they seemingly come straight down underneath the body of the craft? If extending outside the circumference, it was a real physical craft-the straddling of legs better distributed the weight. If they were extended straight down it was hallucinatory, an illusion has no weight.

5.   If the craft was rising from the earth, did it go up on a slant, extremely straight up, or did it flip sharply into the distance and disappear in an instant? If it seemed to go up on a slight or greater slant, it was a real craft. If it shot straight up on the perpendicular rather quickly, or flipped away in an instant, it was illusory.

6.   All physical craft have one feature in common that seems so commonplace that few mention it. All physical craft are perfectly symmetrical in form, whether round, oval, oblongish or whatever. It is a matter of balance. If there is a protrusion it must be symmetrical as well, balancing both "sides" of the craft. Illusory craft often have jutting projections that would throw a physical craft off balance. In a hallucinatory craft, balance has no virtue. (Did you notice projections or asymmetry of the craft?)

7.   Now consider craft rising from the sea, one of the major mysteries many attribute to UFO appearance. All craft seen under the water or rising from the water are semi-corporeal or an illusion. Witness, there is no splash. If there is, a physical craft is in trouble. (Have you witnessed a craft in, under or near the water?)

Semi-corporeality is a real thing, but not the same kind of physical substance as the "nutz-and-boltz" or hardware craft. Not only can the craft be semi-corporeal, but it also can carry semi-corporeal occupants. This is too difficult to explain in these limited pages. We will tell in a subsequent chapter about occupants, and a little more about the physical craft.

Of course all of the above questions imply something more than just average, ordinary experiences, but rather something of constant and impressive examples.

Questions

Scoring yourself from 10 (high) to 1 (low), how well do you think you fit the list of character traits given on the first page of this chapter? If you would rather, have an understanding friend or generous relative score you on these.

Open-mindedness

Investigative nature

Generosity

Concern with world problems

Courage

Endurance, durability

Lovingness and kindness

Do you recall at any time, or several times, making a declaration of intent to help your fellowman or expressed a desire to be of use in the world? Relate as many details as you wish.

How to tell if your experience was a hallucinatory event:

1.   Were there elements of delay between your experience and your memory of it? Relate briefly.

2.   Were you, at any time, during the experience, exposed to strong currents as though of electricity, electrical forces or currents? Relate briefly.

3.   Were there any observations of small circular objects like glowing tennis balls with an intense white glow? Describe briefly.

4.   Were you seemingly impelled toward some person or object as though you wanted to run toward it (or him) and greet or welcome it? Relate briefly.

5.   Were there instances, perhaps more than one, of feelings of dizziness, or a swimming of the head? Describe briefly.

6.   Were there strange forms of any kind that seemed to have no significance or use, something that would be seen, perhaps, in a very modernistic stage setting? Describe.

7.   After the event and you were safely at home, did you feel let down, disappointed, aggrieved, or hopelessly at loose ends?

8.   Did you completely lose sight, during the event, of what time or what day it was?

If the answer to these last eight questions, or at least most of them, is "yes" then your experience was purely hallucinatory due to hypnosis, a very subtle and refined kind of hypnosis. It was intended as a learning experience; the value to become known at a proper time.

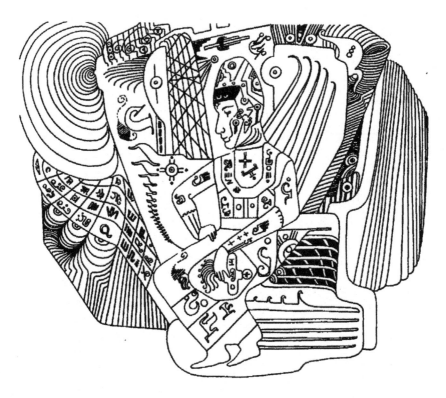

The first act of the initiatory process is to separate the initiate from his communal partners. The personage showed here looks very much alone, indeed rather lonely, as he contemplates the symbols (new ideas) before him.

CHAPTER TWO

Separation

Each contactee's experience is individual and unique, just as he/she is a unique individual. Even though several may have been together at the beginning of an experience, they are soon separated and treated separately.

Close and long study of these individual contacts disclose that each has been carefully planned and directed to suit the mental and emotional state of that particular person. Two or more persons are seldom in close enough harmony of condition that they can both be treated or be expected to react in total unison. A second reason for the individuality of each experience is that it is meant as an induction into an initiatory process which proceeds onward from that time. The first impact is only the beginning.

All initiations follow the same basic formula, of which the first step is to isolate the initiate, somehow cut him out of the herd and to separate him from his communal partners. A contact experience does this first in the singular event, and then in his friends' and neighbors' reaction to his telling of it. He feels alone, broods and worries about his experience.

Years ago Dale Carnegie wrote a book *How to Win Friends and Influence People.* I could write it in a single line; it would not take a book: How to Lose Friends and Alienate People—just try telling them of your UFO experience.

In primitive societies the initiate, usually at puberty, is taken forcibly from the mother, though this is often a ritual force. Thereafter the young novitiate is kept separated for a period of time, sometimes as much as a year, or even more. When the initiation is complete he does not return to his mother; he is now a full-fledged member of the community.

That is what you are being trained to become, but in your case it is not to return to the small social sphere you knew. It is to a larger world-wide community of humanity, or maybe an interplanetary, intergalactic or even a cosmic community. Maybe all of the above. At this point we don't know how far our new communal spirit will extend. But we are on our way.

The fact that you will find no one to listen to your story will further complete the idea of separation. In fear and anxiety you may be driven to acts that seem totally unreasonable to those who do not understand the emotional pain and uncertainties that you struggle with. Everything that happens only serves to separate you more from your former associates. You learn to be secretive, which but cuts you off further. Perhaps you have been warned by those SBs themselves to "tell no one."

If you have ongoing contacts, mental telepathy, night visions or dreams that are too vivid to be ordinary dreams, you will now become emotionally and mentally dependent on your UFO communicants, no matter how they present themselves. Now they are all you have. Marital discords can easily arise at this time.

Play it cool. Be discreet. Don't rub other people's noses in your experience, and most of the frictions will ease.

The SBs know full well how to aggravate and intensify that dependency on them. They will offer bribes, lures, lavishing compliments, even endearments one moment, then putting you through the rigors of another "test," as they like to call them, the next. If you complain of such treatment you get, "It was only a test. Forget it."

I remember complaining that they seemed to build me up one moment only to knock me down the next. This mental treatment was more painful than physical blows. Something would be told one day, which was contradicted on the next; and on the following I was told something totally opposite, until my mind was a pulp, unable to think, which was precisely where those SBs wanted me: a slate wiped clean, waiting for the new writing that was to come.

Whatever your experience has been, or is—a sighting, an observation, an induction (I prefer this to abduction), or ongoing dreams, visions, or telepathic contacts—at the end of the first phase you will find yourself standing very much alone, with no support group, probably not even a confidant at this point.

You will now be taken apart bit by bit, first by the SBs and somewhat later by the investigators and their ubiquitous questionnaires. In this they serve a good purpose but differently than the SBs. The SBs strip you down and expose you to yourself relentlessly, hopefully without harm, certainly as compassionately as they can and still get the job done rather quickly. You will find yourself shredded mentally and shivering in your underwear.

The difference between the SBs and those investigators who are careless and uncaring is that the SBs will spend hours and hours, days and weeks, and even years helping you reconstruct yourself into a more useful function. The uncaring investigators leave you shredded and shivering. The point the SBs are making here is that you need a little TLC in refunctionalizing (I made that word up) yourself.

From here on you will go through many additional experiences, suffer, learn, readjust your mental, emotional and psychological pieces and parts and become a totally independent whole again. If you last that long.

It is not easy. And in the cultural context of today, it is hardly respectable. Are you something of a loner, a free thinker, a rebel? You will have it easier than most.

We have to do it ourselves, but we will be guided, pushed, inspired, shoved, coerced, bribed and even threatened, mostly through bad dreams. Those dreams are not meant to show what is necessarily going to happen in the world, but what could happen if the world of humans does not make some improvements. We are shown the future by *probabilities* only, not unalterable fact. Hang onto that consoling thought! The future we are threatened with is not inevitable, only probable, a potential out of many potentials. The course of events can be changed, by you among others.

You have been separated and cut out of the herd to be retrained and made a useful member of a community as large or larger than this world. It's as simple an answer as that!

Remember—you stated your intention yourself, to help your fellow man. Your UFO experience is the beginning of a response to that plea. How did you expect it to happen? It is not easy and it won't be quick. Be prepared for more of the same or even much worse.

Now we can hear the "Why me?" syndrome. And a self-analysis follows: "What have I done to draw their attention? Who am I?

What am I that they should single me out? What do I have that they want?"

This process of self-analysis is the beginning of a long chore. You will constantly be asking yourself all sorts of impertinent questions about yourself, until you have completely emptied out all those nooks and crannies of things you wanted to forget, of little secrets about yourself that you didn't want to know, of little faults and failures you didn't want to admit. A total catharsis and an exercise in being honest with yourself, the self-questioning will go on until you are completely, totally, strictly honest, and it will go on even as many other events are happening over the ensuing months and years. It means a mental cleansing that is too often a mental torture, or at least a private embarrassment. After so long a time it gets easier, even habitual, and you learn to accept it, not with some neurotic self-pity, but with a great deal of humor at how silly you can be.

While casting about for a good illustration of the separation principle, I came across *Abducted—Confrontation with Beings from Outer Space* by Coral and Jim Lorenzen, who conducted research for APRO—the Aerial Phenomenon Research Organization. It contained in good detail the story of three women contactees, indeed abductees: Louise Smith, Mona Stafford, and Elaine Thomas of Liberty, Kentucky. This abduction took place on January 6, 1976. It took some period of time until details of their experiences were brought out under hypnosis. To quote, "Each woman seemed to experience the impression that she had been taken out of the car and placed elsewhere without her friends." Each went through an individual and separate kind of examination and each thought they were in a different kind of place. This points up once more the idea that each experience is planned for each individual according to his or her psychological condition and beliefs. It is not germane to our cause to go more deeply into their experiences at this time.

Another facet the Lorenzens brought out in this story was the apparent lack of willingness of some of the investigators on the scene to want to share information. If only everyone were willing to share their information and collaborate toward some program of interpretation, the whole mystery would not take so long to unravel. If they are too anxious to sit on their material until they can hatch the whole thing by themselves, it is going to take a bit longer, maybe forever.

There may be some preliminary contacts of one kind or another before the big vital one could take place, and the big one could be broken into segments and followed by other contacts, various contacts of comparable vitality. For each contactee the planned experience was patterned for himself according to the beliefs and habits he already had, i.e., *according* to what he would listen to. And this is why single contactees have one experience rather than two or three at once. Only in a few cases where a number are of the same pattern of belief—or closely allied ones—are there vital contacts involving more than one contactee at a time.

In the case of the three women from Liberty, Kentucky, all three were regular church goers, lived in the same community, were interested in art and seemed to have similar backgrounds and tastes. They were close together in their ages, 35, 44, and 48, and were all responsible family members.

According to the SBs, questions such as these had to be answered before contact could be made:

- What was the potential contactee able to accept as a factual event?
- What knowledge did he have that would permit him to come to some acceptance of that event?
- How long would he rely on his own power to accept that event? How soon would he seek help?
- How many times would it be necessary to repeat happenings of various kinds before he would completely immerse himself in the acceptance, assimilation and exposition of the event or events?
- What factors in his education or cultural background would keep him from acceptance and belief in his experience?
- How much emotional enhancement would have to be brought to bear to make him receptive to the UFO message?
- On what beliefs would his negative attitudes be based?
- What other allied beliefs bolstered up these beliefs basic to his negativism?

- For what length of time had he maintained these attitudes?
- Were those beliefs traditional to his cultural background? Within his family only? From his personal understanding only? Or what combination of these?
- Who besides himself in his immediate lifehood subscribed to similar beliefs?
- Were his beliefs reinforced by any personal experience in his past?
- Was there an ongoing enhancement of these basic beliefs in the present?
- Were influences being brought to bear on him that might change, modify, or increase these particular beliefs? How often did he overtly make an expression of his beliefs? (Each incident would strengthen his negativism.)
- Who besides himself actively contributed to his negativism? (A personal contributor, a publication or other media.)
- What inner emotions, fears or desires helped sustain these beliefs?
- Was there some other psychological factor within himself that made those beliefs necessary to his acceptance of self?
- Was this psychological factor consistently reinforced by frequent events?
- Who, besides himself, contributed to that psychological factor?
- What was his belief and attitude concerning the following?
  Ghosts
  Spirits of the deceased
  Life after death
  Reincarnation
  Nature spirits
  Fairies, nymphs, diyads, *etc.*
  Gods and Goddesses of the mythologies
  Satan and demons

God

Angels

Prophets

Messiahs

Purpose of Humanity. Evolution

Astrology

Traditional religions in general

Goblins, trolls, leprechauns and allied creatures

Witches and warlocks.

- To what extent did he fantasize?
- Did he accept as possible, probable or true the products of his fantasies?
- How much did he believe in his dreams?
- How well could he recall his dreams?
- By what method did he interpret his dreams?
- What talisman of good fortune did he believe in?
- What omens of misfortune did he believe in?
- Did he wear on his person any charm or amulet to attract good luck or ward off bad? And how deeply did he actually believe in the efficacy of these?
- Did he believe humans could control or manipulate unseen powers and forces? How deeply did he believe?
- What was his belief in or attitude toward divine reward and punishment? Appeasement of gods? Acts of contrition?
- Did he believe in miracles and miraculous events?
- Did he believe humans could incite miracles, and by what means?
- Did he ever attend seances, spiritual gatherings, spiritualist churches or experiment in psychic phenomena?
- How profound was his belief in such activities? Was his interest curiosity only or a fervent belief?
- If any "results" were obtained, how eagerly did he accept or vehemently deny the worth of such results?
- Was such activity fostered/bolstered by others, or did he research alone?
- How cautious or secretive was he in speaking to others of his activities and results?

- What were his expectations in engaging in such activities? Did he expect great monetary rewards or riches? Did he look for power through special knowledge?
- How well trained was he in study disciplines?
- How industriously did he study?
- How patient/impatient was he relative to possible results?
- How much disappointment could he accept and still be willing to go ahead?
- Was he resilient and flexible enough to allow his beliefs to grow or to refine or modify them with time and experience?
- Were his beliefs so ingrained and adamant that he could not cope with unusual experiences but would break or shatter emotionally or mentally?
- Was he open-minded enough to give a new idea or an extension or modification of an old one a chance to be heard and considered?
- Was he analytical enough to distill the value of an experience?
- Was he open-hearted enough to cooperate and share new knowledge with others?
- Was his mental and spiritual energy and stamina sufficient to cope with the activities necessary relative to the experience of contact?
- Would his preconceived ideas and beliefs allow him to derive the greatest possible benefit from his contact experience, or would the entire episode be a waste of time and energy (for the SBs)?

And that, dear contactee, is how well those SBs studied and knew you before they made that big contact!

As for being alone: your former associates do not reject you because they hate you. You have shown them an *unknown* and they don't want to think about it. Those who reject you are more afraid than you are. You are courageous, or you never would have been chosen by those SBs to go through such ordeals. The SBs know. I know. You know. And hundreds and hundreds of contactees out there know, many of whom have never spoken up. Yet.

Who really listens and helps us in response? Few! Few! There are those who will squeeze every drop of information out of you and leave you bone dry, burning with thirst on the desert.

If you and I were really crazy, why would we work so hard and give so much hope to help others? Truly "crazy" people live in their own self-constructed inner world and have no sense of responsibility or concern for their fellow man. They do not go about in logical ways to put that concern into action. Let that be the criterion!

"By their works ye shall know them."

Take heart. You are not alone. You are not crazy. Time will bring the proof. *Hang Tough!*

Questions

1.   At the time of your experience were you in very good health, good health, or poor health?

2.   Before your sighting or confrontation, something strange, accompanied by a strong emotion, came into your mind. What was it like? Like a warning, a message, a premonition, an apprehension or dread, a feeling of grief, an expectation, a sudden concern for someone, a vast longing, a regret, a sudden joy or ecstasy, a feeling there was a problem you must solve or a duty you must perform, or any other strong feeling or thought? Describe fully. For example, just before the event you may have noticed a sudden strangeness in the atmosphere: a sense of still, vast quiet; rushing air without observable wind; a strange overall glow if at night, or if in day a strong sensation of gathering gloom; feelings of a wave of something passing through self, not as strong as a vibration, just a swaying of the inner self; sudden catching and holding of breath, or almost non-breathing, a sensation of being surrounded by pinpoints of lights, smaller than fireflies and white rather than yellow; any other strange physical sensation or atmospheric observation.

3.   On your first glimpse of the UFO or the occupants what strong feeling, emotion, fear, disbelief or curiosity did you feel?

4.   As events progressed, did a feeling persist that you had been through this before, or had seen this object or this person before, and what was the exact "before" as you remember it?

5.   Did any of the occupants seem somehow like "old friends" to you? Describe fully.

6.   What opportunity have you had for studying psychic phenomena? (Here the opportunities are the vital factor.)

7.   Do you habitually, or sometimes, or never—

   Fantasize?

   Read science fiction?

   See space movies or space programs on TV?

   Study psychic or occult literature?

   Peruse UFO literature?

   Contemplate suicide?

   Fear going insane?

   Prophesy doom?

   Expect the end of the world?

8.   Do you—

          Anticipate the Battle of Armageddon?

          Believe in Satan or Hell?

9.   Have you ever seen, or wanted to see—

          Fairies, gnomes, elves?

          Mythological persons or creatures?

          Outer space beings?

10.   Are you currently worried about—

          The future of Humanity?

          The course of civilization?

          Life after death?

          The reality of God?

11.   Are you looking for aid from—

          Divine intervention?

          Religious philosophy?

          Governmental regulations?

          Science, technology, education?

          Outer space beings?

12.   Describe the manner in which you found yourself separated from others during your initial major experience. Were you alone, or were you separated in some manner?

13.   Describe reactions of your friends and associates when you tried to tell your story.

14.   As time went on, did you find yourself growing apart from former associates and spending more time alone? Describe as fully as you like.

15.   Do you wish with all your heart that you could do something to better Earth conditions?

16.   Have you given much constructive thought to ways in which the world could be made better if only...?

17.   Do you feel you might have an important part to play in coming events?

18.   If an opportunity arose to do some task, large or small, to make all mankind healthier or happier and the earth a better place to live, would you sacrifice for it? Everything—much—a little?

19.   Have you a particular idea, thought, writing, information, theory, plan or any such construct or ability that you would put into effect for such purposes, given the opportunity?

These last few items are some of the things those SBs are testing you for, trying to find out what you want to do, what you can do, how much you are willing to do, where your best talents and opportunities lie and what is best in line for your own welfare and happiness. Now does it begin to make sense?

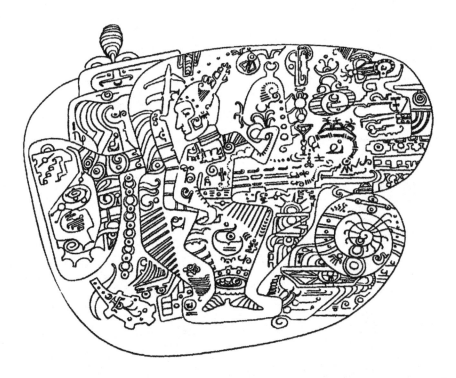

Initiates, and in our case, contactees, about nine times out of ten are led into, or introduced into a round enclosure. This might be a round or oval room, even a squarish room with round corners. Or they may have their sighting from a round irrigated field, a ballpark or a race track. Even a car would answer this description well enough.

Again we see the spiral of ascent the symbol of initiation on the lower right, as well as the snail-like creature on the far left. This Personage holds a plant, symbol of re-growth in his hand.

CHAPTER THREE

Round Enclosure

In the second step of any initiation, the individual is led or somehow lured into a round enclosure, or space, although it may be divided off only by a circle of stones. An observation from a car recognizes the shape of the vehicle as sufficiently answerable to that description.

If there is an abduction, nine times out of ten the contactee will report that he was taken into a round or oval room, a squarish room with the corners rounded off, or a "vaulted" room.

If there was an observation of craft only, the observer may have been standing in a field irrigated in the round pattern, or a ball field which, with its stands and bleachers would appear rounded, or even in a racetrack!

The circle or round enclosure indicates a place of new beginnings. Actually, it represents the womb from which life will spring anew after a gestation period. To the initiate, the gestation period is the time of study and change that takes place after his induction into the event.

In very primitive societies, the round enclosure was often a specially constructed hut, or sometimes a cave, or even a compound where the novitiate was kept for a period of study and learning, often up to a year, and sometimes much longer. In more sophisticated societies the round enclosure may be no more than a circle drawn on the floor, the magic circle.

In UFO experience, the contactee cannot be kept for such a period, but in an essential sense he is kept in contact for a year, or two or ten, or for a lifetime! In the contactee experience you have entered into a new condition and a new direction of life.

Before there can be actual birth to the new life, there must be death to the old. This is represented in the blacking out of memory of the event for a period. It is a time of forgetting many things, not just the contact experience. The contactee will complain, "I just can't seem to remember anything anymore." This blackout period also gives time for changes within the person to take place that will not meet with the same amount of resistance that would be given if all memory were intact. He is being inwardly changed without realizing what is happening.

The changes he makes in his outer life during this period will seem to be entirely of his own choosing. His free will to do or not to do cannot be tampered with, but he is shoved and nudged into certain directions he otherwise might not have noticed. It is a time of incredible coincidences. It is a time of meeting people who will become very important in his future and a time of finding himself doing things he never believed possible.

He himself gives "death" to his old life without realizing what it all means. This does not indicate that he chucks everything and takes off with a knapsack for Tahiti. It means finding a delicate and tenuous balance between the old and new, re-analyzing his values and making definite and articulate choices.

The first act of initiation imitates or suggests an experience of death. The novice is thrust with some violence into the unknown and into the presence of beings that inspire awe and terror.

The break that this engenders with one's former life is absolute; there is no going back. One does not forget the experience ever, although the memory of it is blocked out for a period. It is timed to reappear when the novice is "ready," i.e., when he or she has assimilated certain ideas, not by memorizing rules, but by living, in action, certain experiences that qualify him or her for remembrance. The time of forgetfulness, the blocking out, is the time of death of the old and the gestation of the new.

Other rituals at the time of the induction into initiation can be ritual nudity and the drawing of blood. These ritual observances have been experienced in many a UFO-enforced induction. The nudity and taking of blood may be for more than one purpose, but the initiatory meaning is by no means thus invalidated.

The time of induction is therefore the end of a natural or "innocent" way of being, the end of blindness and irresponsibility. The mode of being changes to the awakened and knowledgeable, a cultural man evolved from the natural. This cultural change and mode is activated by those SBs who in this instance are truly Superior Beings in knowledge and the use of psychic powers. In their activities we come to the second definition of SB—those Sons of Bs—for they put us through experiences we willingly never would have chosen for ourselves.

Yet, in the end, we come out victorious, for we have been hurried through an evolution of being that we never could have reached in our own puttering, blind way. Which makes us wonder, why the hurry? Why are we being rushed along the path to real Manness or real Womanness from the historical Childness of our past?

Before our planet can be changed to a place of peace, beauty and justice, the humans inhabiting it must first change, and then the outer change can take place, and only then. Before we blow our planet and ourselves to smithereens, destroy every atom of plant and animal life, poison the last breath of sweet air or the last sip of pure water—all of which we seem to be well on the way to doing—we must change our inner selves. We must want to change, strive to change, accept change, and accept those who are trying in their own inimitable way to help us find a way of change.

How difficult their task must be when so few are willing to admit they are even real. How many thousands of hours have they spent in our behalf? How much precious information have they given that has fallen on barren ground? Why should they even want to help? Why not withdraw in disgust and leave us to our fate? Let us at least listen to what they have to say. Even if they are not real, somehow they speak well and to the point!

As a contactee you have been chosen to help in this endeavor. But first, we must find some sense in what is going on here. How can we help if we understand nothing? I do believe they could have been a little more explicit sometimes!

You may suffer terrors and ordeals. You may be called upon to make sacrifices that hurt. You may be sent on seemingly pointless journeys, and you may never be rich, famous or endowed with perpetual youth. If you are a bonafide contactee, they already knew these would not be your life goals. Though a little of such rewards would be welcome, we cannot deny that! I keep telling them, "If you would only make my way a little easier, I could produce more." I wish they'd listen!

Speaking of time, this seems as good a time as any to speak a little on that subject. Certainly one of the larger mysteries of the UFO experience is their use of time factors and their sometimes total lack of comprehension as to our measurement of time.

First, they are not as uncomprehending as they pretend. They are trying to make us concentrate on the idea of time, not by telling us to do so, but by confusing us. In our confusion, we think.

After an experience with some SBs in 1954, a Frenchman was asked, "What time is it?"

The man looked at his watch. "It is two-thirty." (Actually it was 2:30:40) "You lie," was the response. "It is four o'clock!" This was not intended as an impertinence. It was meant to say. "Time! Think time! Time is not the same for everyone. Think about time!"

I have been thinking, and though the model I draw is in no way perfect, I truly believe it is reaching in the direction of a verbal reality. No doubt mathematics could say it more precisely, but since I can't keep my checkbook straight, I am stuck with words.

When we talk about "conditions of reality" we are really talking about *time* conditions as they relate to consciousness.

Consciousness and Time

- Subconscious: buried time, inert time, smothered time. Time is squashed by the weight of a new event. The residue of the past is so compacted it is hard to pull out any time. When we do, we call it memory.

- Conscious: physical or mechanistic time, measured by the motion of the earth turning on its axis and the motion of the planet revolving about its sun. This gives us day and night, hours, seasons and the notions of sequence and duration.

- Super-conscious: non-time. Relationships of motions of galaxies within the universe. This motion is constant, therefore it is "apparent" as non-time. Measurements just don't count. It is within the super-consciousness that psychic phenomena takes place (along with much else). When we perfect the idea of non-time, we can manipulate psychic events just as the SBs do. We have made an approach in hypnosis. Hypnosis does not control the mind of the subject, it releases the mind into non-time. Here it can roam freely without any restriction of mechanistic earth time.

- Supra-conscious: expansion of everything in the universe at the same rate: all is relative. It seems motionless, and comparative sizes and distances remain the same. Here time is as much space as time, or better said, time and space become interchangeable.

The SBs do not work within the framework of mechanistic time except when they interact with Earthlings, who are imprisoned by it. The SB work is carried out by many different factions. But any delay on the part of one faction holds back the work for all. Each has to try to keep up and sometimes wait for the others. The only way so vast a program could work with so many different ideas of time, is through synchronous event...synchronicity, not an actual time table.

The SBs and their planners have not invented synchronicity; they simply use this very natural process to order their events and the coming together of events.

To understand the need for synchronicity as used by the SBs or whoever plan their activities, we must know that there is a vast variety of workers, a vast variety of tasks and an equally vast variety of conditions and circumstances under which the work is done. A time schedule could not possibly control it. When all factors come together properly, the event occurs.

The SBs tell me that these points are also important:

1. Various factions do not necessarily know any other faction or any other part of the larger plan than their own. They obey instructions and may not even know the final purpose of the instructions they are carrying out. They have faith and obey and possibly only have enough information to allow a necessary flexibility.

2. Overall the workers come from widely separated places and are various types of beings, some as alien to each other as they are to us.

3. Within each faction each personage is as unique an individual as among ourselves, with various personalities and manners of doing things. (Except for some of the little big-heads, or grays, who are cloned and semi-programmed?)

4. There are an infinite number of jobs to be done, each with its own requirements.

5. If several factions have personal contacts or simply parallel work, or their work is contingent upon that of a "neighboring" faction, there can be conflicts and delays. Various factions are not always agreeable to each other.

6. While all work toward a common end and with a common purpose, there are discords, jealousies and variances of viewpoints and judgments.

7.   Any delaying fumble within one faction creates a chain of delay everywhere resulting in nervous impatience and flaring tempers.

The above observations are only common sense, the same factors would hold true with us in similar circumstances. I believe these factors not only explain the need for use of synchronicity but also help to explain the many discrepancies in contactee reports. It is a vast project, and the variances are equally vast.

Questions

1.   Where were you at onset of the event?

    Were you in a car?

    A rounded field?

    A ball park?

    A race track?

    Another circular, oval or semi-circular place?

2.   If taken aboard a craft, what was the shape of the room in which you spent most of the time?

3.   Did you have memory trouble after the event?

4.   How long after the experience did you have recall?

5.   Did you have dreams relative to the event before total recall?

6.   Did your recall come naturally, or was hypnosis a factor? Describe.

7.   Was divesting of garments a factor in the event?

8.   Was blood taken, and if so, what was the reason given?

9. Was disorientation of time, or time in any way, a factor in the event?

The pilot is speaking into a communications device. It looks almost like a button telephone. Just above is a camera or a viewing instrument. The exquisite bird on the upper right is the Phoenix, symbol of re-birth. Note also the inverted triangle figure on the bird's wing and the eye above it. The inverted triangle means "from above or from the sky," not necessarily "Heaven." The "sky" has its eye on us! (Perhaps intended for "The eye of Horus")

Things and Symbols Seen

According to the information given by the SBs themselves, there are eight basic types of craft, with many sub-types, usually experimental, but there are countless more "seen" that are actually psychic manifestations or illusions.

Eight Types of Craft

1. Circular with flattish dome
2. Elongated cylinders, sometimes with blunt ends
3. Like wings swept back, almost touching, looking somewhat like doughnuts if glimpsed briefly
4. Like two saucers, top one inverted, no dome
5. Balls or circles of light or flame, floating, whirling, spinning, or rushing
6. Trapezoid (rare)
7. Cone shape with truncated bottom, (also rare)
8. Boomerang, a newer experimental one

"These are the basic hardware craft. There are many minor variations. They travel mostly through a time differential but come through space also. That is, part of their journey is also through space. They use anti-magnetic force, not anti-gravity, though they can exert such force that gravity is overcome.

"We can deliberately maneuver any hardware craft to make it appear like anything, and we often do. It can appear to the viewer as a shooting star, a full moon, a moonrise, or a will o' the wisp. Psychically through hypnosis we affect, not the craft, but the mind of the viewer. Craft other than the eight basic types and their minor extensions are almost certain to be induced hallucinations."

By now it must seem self-evident that the SBs do not all come to us from one place, nor from one period of time, nor come in a like manner, nor are they all of one type of being.

Some are as physical and corporeal as ourselves; some come as psychic extensions of corporeal beings; and some are almost pure-energy existences that can come in any form they choose, from whirligigs to human beings. Touch one of these humans and your hand goes right through him. Very upsetting. He may fade out before your eyes even as you stare at him. Very disconcerting. Or his human features may dissolve and an animal or bird head appear in its place. Scary as hell. They are full of tricks, millions of them. But they are each for a purpose. We are *not* to take them at face value. We should have learned by this time that a rose is *not* a rose is a rose where SBs are concerned. Take them as symbols, as metaphors, even as parables, just don't take them as fact. To find the meanings behind all this charade we must go—to our own *past.*

"Stop looking at the stars and start looking at the earth beneath your feet," I was told with some vehemence. Archaeology? Ancient civilizations? At least ancient symbols, languages, legends, myths and traditions. There is the real meat. It is in our past, of which we have forgotten too much, that we must look to discover the meanings, the interpretations of all those disguises in which they come to us.

So the SBs continue: "We have described the manner in which you may tell our craft from an illusion. Now we do the same for the occupants."

Types of Craft Occupants

Humans, very much like yourselves of the Earth's builds and appearances. (Some of us come from the same roots.) All will appear young to middle-aged, though their actual ages vary greatly.

Humans much like yourselves, but with some obvious though not great differences, such as coloring of hair or eyes, or larger size, much taller or extremely slender.

Those you call humanoid. These are true humans, as true as yourselves, but with great differences in bodily contours, facial features, differences of hands or feet, strange colored skin or lack of hair, *etc.* These are the workers, not directors or scientists. They follow explicit directions, though they have great patience and can try several courses of action if one is blocked. They are very intelligent, but not originators. Some of these have been cloned, no others ever have been or will be. A great error was recognized.

Those humanoid types who seem almost robot-like with jerky motions. These are preprogrammed to carry out, almost mechanically, certain exact plans. They do not deviate from their course, regardless. Their way is inexorable. They are not supposed to have actual or close contact with Earthlings.

Robots, preprogrammed for certain activities, not very useful in exploration of Earth. Too much of the unexpected arises, for which they have no programming.

Types fantastically different from earth humans, but seemingly alive and intelligent with purposeful action and intent.

(We will talk more about the occupants in Chapter 5.)

If, as we have said, the SBs are giving us not actuality, but symbols and ideas in the contactee experience, what of the objective surface factors? What kind of graphic portrayal or dioramic event is encountered? Why, and how?

Subjects Contained in Graphical Portrayals of Craft Experiences

1. UFO types of craft
2. Occupant types
3. Interior of craft
4. Propulsion devices
5. Maps, diagrams, charts
6. Articles of interaction

Subjects Contained in Graphical Portrayals of Non-Craft

Experiences

1. Background area of experience
2. Alien or device encountered
3. Emotional atmosphere of encounter
4. Presentation methods
5. Messages, information, records
6. Any physical phenomena

True enough, 10,000 repetitions of the same or similar scenes and portrayals and devices do not prove their truth, but it does prove that the contactee experience is true and that the UFO communicators are trying to get across some definite propaganda. For some reason the UFO occupants are trying to make us believe these observations and explanations are so and are using incredible amounts of their own time and trouble to do so. But here we are investigating the contactee experience, not the SBs integrity, and we ask that this be held in mind as we continue.

Now we interpret some symbols as used by and defined by the SBs. In Chapter 1 of Part II we mentioned the story of Betty Andreasson and outlined her initiatory ordeals. Here are a few more symbols of her journey:

In the distance and to one side she saw domes as edifices in a city. The domes were presented as "edifices of knowledge." The fact that they were domes indicated knowledge that had been worn in time, i.e., traditional knowledge. They were off to one side to imply that the traditional knowledge should be laid aside at this point. Something new was to occur.

The blue-green effect or the mingling of blue and green was to remind her that at all times her experiences were based on natural progression, the co-mingling was the blue of the sky and green of the earth, all nature. Seeing the sea off to one side represented origins. Always in any context the sea represents origins.

A pyramid of any kind in any place means a place of initiation. The pyramid may be used for other purposes, and it may have deeper meanings, but primarily it represents a place of initiation.

It is generally believed that the ancient people from whom these symbols derived were sun worshipers. Taint so. They were God worshipers but utilized the sun as the most real and awesome aspect of his power and energy. The sun represented the radiance, power and constancy of God. It was only in much, much later times that the meaning was perverted into worship of the sun itself.

The whirling tunnel indicated that changes were taking place. The unenlightened way was changing into an enlightened way. It would take time for the meaning to become known.

She glided with her guides along a narrow track. This is just what it would seem to be, keeping to the "straight and narrow."

Her feet glided without motion. This indicates the effortless fway to the light is to stick to the right path as shown by the guides.

Another fact to mention here before we go on to other symbols was that Betty constantly complained of the heaviness of her feet and limbs. Recall that Betty was in a semi- corporeal state during her adventure. To a person in such a state, any object in the same state would be just as solid and hard as a material effect against a corporeal body. However, any pure energy effect against a semi-corporeal body or against a body when its mind is in a state of illusion would affect more strongly or violently than if it were normally corporeal. This is why pure energy (thought) directed to Betty's body to hold it under control was sensed by her as a very heavy weight or a super strong force.

Now for the symbols that you, as a contactee, have been given. As each event was specifically planned for a unique individual, only he or she can adequately interpret the meaning of such symbols. Perhaps an example can show what I mean more quickly than exposition:

Let us imagine that three different men have reported seeing "A man in armor." We cannot add three suits of armor and get one meaning. We have to ask each contactee in turn: "What does a man in armor mean to you? Does it suggest something from your past?"

The first man answers, "King Arthur's Court."

"What does that mean to you? How do you feel about King Arthur's Court?"

"When I was little, my grandmother read to me about the Knights of the Round Table. I wished there were still knights, so I could grow up and be one, and fight against evil; fight for what is right?"

"What are you doing now to fight for what is right?"

"Well, nothing. I dropped out of law school because it took too long, and I needed to make money now."

"Could the man in armor have been telling you to go back to law school, even if it meant night school, anything, so you could fight for justice?"

The second man responded to the first question:

"When I was still fairly young, I used to spend my summers with my grandparents in England. In the library were two suits of armor. I was forbidden to touch them. One day I was fooling around, knocked one over and it practically disintegrated. I thought it was so old and decrepit it could not have any value, but I was severely impressed that we must preserve things that can never be replaced."

"Would that admonition mean anything in your present?"

"Come to think of it, yes. I am in the logging business and right now I am engaged in a big hassle with some busy body group that is trying to keep me from cutting trees on my own domain. They say this is virgin timber, some of the trees nearly a thousand years old."

"Doesn't that recall the admonition learned from a suit of armor? Preserve the irreplaceable?"

The third man says:

"Some of my ancestors were in the Crusades. I used to think the crusades would still be around when I grew up and I could go on one."

"Are you on a crusade?"

"No, but I've thought sometimes about joining something like Greenpeace or 'Save the Sea Lions' or something like that."

"Go ahead. That is what the man in armor was telling you. Join a crusade, Greenpeace, or whatever a crusade means to you now."

So we have three different visions of practically the same thing, men in suits of armor, but three distinctly different messages. That is why we need to know the psychological impact of a UFO on a contactee and also know something of his cultural background. Only he or she can tell us.

In the UFO event we are not given exhortations, we are given experiences, even the psychically manifested clues are "actual" in their own sense, and the things they show us, the events they put us through, are symbolic pictures that we are meant to observe, analyze and understand. We are simply having called to our attention the "hidden side of things" that can, in our present state of non-awareness, be given to us only symbolically and metaphorically. The purpose would seem to be to raise our level of awareness, to make us wake up and *think.*

The following are symbols devised by the SBs for general use when specific meanings are not needed for specific contactees. These are not necessarily traditional.

Symbols Used by SBs

OBJECTS

- Rose: Power, particularly mental power, i.e., the ability to comprehend.
- Flame: Spirit.
- Fruit: Passion.
- Wheat: Reward.
- Spear: Speed or haste.
- Crystal: Energy of creativity.
- Prisms: Beauty.
- Egg: Pristine beginnings.
- Drooping flower: Ailment or remedy.
- Light: Knowledge of Reality.
- Mirror—looking into: Recall of self; total awareness of self.
- Sarcophagus: Laying aside earthly considerations; passing into spirit.
- Lightning bolt: Emergency
    On sleeve of uniform: Emergency crews, trouble shooters.
- Sun: Life force.
- Food or drink: Knowledge.
- Shower, bath or dousing: Acceptance as initiands, baptism, spiritual cleansing.
- Change of clothing: Change of life attitudes.
- Sky maps or sea charts: Other dimensions of being.
- Bits and pieces of something scattered: Need to organize thinking and activities.
- Scientific apparatus: A statement, "Take this for real, no magic here."

PLACES

- Sea: Origins.
- Tunnel: Unenlightened ways.
- Round opening to pass through: Regeneration.
- Anything whirling: Changes taking place.
- Wisps of vapor or fog: Need to focus attention.

GEOMETRIC SHAPES

- Triangle:

Pertains to psychic nature if point is up-from earth.

If point is down-from sky (not necessarily from heaven.)

- Two opposing triangles interlaced, the so-called Star of David: Co-operation of earth and sky (not necessarily from heaven.)
- Cross: Struggle or mission.
- Spirals: A new beginning: from lower to higher; symbol of initiation.
- Right hand crescent: The mystery planet.
- Square: Mechanistic space. (Our kind of space.)
- Square intersected by two horizontal lines: Space travel.
- Diamond: Mechanistic time. (Our kind of time.)
- Diamond intersected by X: Time travel.
- Circle, closed: Star, planet, or any heavenly body.
- Circle, open at top: Inter-communication between planets.
- Circle intersected by X: Interaction of planets.
- Several circles interlaced: Collaboration of planets.
- Cross within circle: Inner-planetary struggles, difficulties, disasters.
- Circle with two spraddled legs below: Man.
- Circle within two such legs: Woman.
- A circle pierced by two such legs: Humanity.
- Circle with triangle inside: Other dimensions than physical within a planet.
- Cones: Concentration of power or energy.
- Globes or balls: Worlds.
- Swastika: Its earliest meaning was earth rotating on its axis. The four equal arms are the four directions. Add the "legs" running, and the directions are running around themselves, that is, rotating. (Yes, indeed, the earliest civilizations knew the earth rotated on its axis. Ask the Dogons! The knowledge was subsequently smothered and lost.)

COLORS

- Green: Color of life.
- Red: Color of death.
- Black: Color of regeneration. Also can mean something hidden, unknown, depending on manner of use.
- White: Color of ignorance.
- Yellow: Color of energy.
- Blue: Color of ecstasy.
- Violet: Color of infancy.
- Orange: Color of dispute.

ORIENTATIONS

- Right side of any symbol: Positive or affirmative side.
- Left side of any symbol: Negative or denial side.
- Right half of stylized tree: Disaster or disaster equipment.
- Left half of stylized tree: Disaster averted, or disaster information.
- Arc, opening downward: Physical universe.
- Arc, opening upward: "Unseen" universe.

BEINGS

- Flying serpent: Secular knowledge.
    If seen on chest of costume—a scientist.
    If seen on sleeve of uniform—a worker for a scientist.
- Phoenix: Re-birth.
    If seen on chest of costume (robe)—spiritual advisor.
        If seen on sleeve of uniform—a worker for a priest.
    (Herodotus described the painting of the Phoenix that he saw in Egypt as resembling an eagle. Later Egypt turned the symbol into a heron; China used a pheasant. Still others use the peacock).
- Bird in flight: Advancement.
- Lion: Ruler, ruling class, chief.
- Lion—recumbent with paws crossed: Secret.
- Persons wearing robes with any insignia: Initiated ones.
- Persons wearing deep head coverings like veils or cowls: those going through initiation, not yet fully initiated.
- Birds: Flight, travel through air, and by extension through space.
- Animals: Necessity to satisfy physiological demands, food, drink, etc.
- Mythological beings or literary figures: Whatever they represent to the particular contactee who sees them.

Both the so-called Star of David and the Swastika are very ancient symbols, the original meanings lost in unremembered places. This is why those SBs lead contactees into studying ancient civilizations, so that basic meanings can be discovered, along with a multitude of other forgotten things.

Perhaps in the beginning of their extended association with Earthlings, the SBs did not realize how much we had lost of our own antiquity, how much we did not recall. They based their symbols on our own past. It is we who fail to remember the truly ancient meanings.

Questions

1.   Describe any UFO which you saw or were on and tell about your experience relative to the craft in detail. Include any markings or insignia seen on craft or inside, and tell where. Describe interior in detail.

2. Were any strange objects seen inside or outside of craft like:

balls of light?

whirling objects?

pinwheels?

(These are forms of "energy existences".)

Describe their appearance and detail actions. Sketch if possible, or continue description.

3.   Describe in detail any objects you might have seen that could have had symbolic meaning or intent.

4.   Describe in detail the appearance of any alien or occupant you have seen. Include a description of any insignia on clothing, and type of clothing.

5.   Describe in detail any event or symbol that seemed to have been devised specifically for you and tell how it relates first to your past, and secondly to your present. You should find this interesting, even fun!

Tutors, mentors, or spiritual guides are given to the contactee to help him learn all he must. For each contactee this is an individual process, but all follow certain outlines of study. In some primitive societies the tutor or instructor always wore a mask, thus symbolizing the return of the mythical ancestors who taught the various arts in the beginning.

CHAPTER FIVE

Tutors

I said we would talk more about occupants in this chapter, so let's get that out of the way first.

The type of occupant is considerably more important than the type of UFO. The latter is, after all, a mechanism, or a reasonable facsimile thereof, an instrument derived from the science and technology of the occupants or their masters. This holds true if the craft was "nutz-and-boltz", a "psychic" type or an induced hallucination. The idea of any of them is a scientific and technological statement of possibility.

It is the revelation of the occupants, not the craft that exposes their motivation, intent and purpose. One wonders why so much importance is attached to the types of craft, propulsion systems, even origins, when the final intent, the great meaning of it all, can only be exposed through contact with the *minds* that are behind it all.

The first factor of curiosity should be those personages who communicate. Who are *they?* What are *their* purposes? Are these totally revealed through their words, or are their words sparse, unrevealing, obscurant or deceptive? Are they masters or workers, instructors or obedients, humans or robots, cyborgs or slaves or even hallucinations?

Occupants must be studied from such viewpoints as these, not from how many fingers they had, what clothing they wore, or how they glided, walked or floated, though all these are necessary observations. Such details are only of momentary importance, a recognition factor. Beyond that they tell us little.

We must somehow break away from this totally static area of research and study the occupants from the question of their seeming importance in the overall picture and their individual motivation. This will lead us in the direction of discovery of the hierarchy of personages involved, and hopefully and eventually the final purpose of the overall plan. This will be a slow road to follow, composed of many steps, stops and much uncertainty, but it will lead into the future of final discovery.

Such study of the occupants will not be dependent on the physical aspects and their repetitions, but on the revelations, intended or not, of the way the aliens are thinking about the situation, the contactee and their own involvement.

Study the occupant or alien, no matter what his appearance from the human aspect, as though he were another human being with whom you wanted to become better acquainted. Does he seem glad, sad, impatient, disdainful, compliant, dismayed, rebellious or any one of a thousand other things?

Such a study will lead you into their minds, and behind these will be discovered the minds that planned it all, the master minds that either dare not or cannot be seen in themselves.

Once you have been inducted into the UFO mysteries you may anticipate any number of the following:

What Contactees Can Expect

- Participation in a baptism of one form or another, some quite obscure.
- Appearance of a tutor, mentor, guide, or instructor, perhaps several at first, but eventually settling down to one.
- Participation in disciplines, vows, rituals and ordeals, including fasts, vigils, journeys, quests and sacrifices.
- Learning of traditions, ancient languages, myths and symbols. This will concentrate on ancient civilizations, Sumer, Egypt, Peru, Central America, Mayans and Southwest American Indians.
- Acceptance of tasks in varying degrees of difficulty, each successively more difficult but never impossible.
- Receiving revelations of certain valuable information or of some of the secrets behind the ongoing experiences.
- Development of special talents or abilities, perhaps the taking up again of creative work abandoned in the past.
- Gaining, in various ways, more self-confidence, better working habits and more direction.

Some of the ordeals they can think up are horrendous. Through it all remember that you are responsible for yourself, for your own behavior and your own soul. If their requests are too outlandish for you to approve, if it involves sacrificing your basic responsibilities or taking the last cent from the family cookie jar, tell them to go soak their heads. They won't die or even hold it against you. They will simply back off and figure another way to get what they want at less cost to you. If you don't tell them where you stand on a specific point, they won't really know.

They test you for your loyalties to your already acquired responsibilities. If you neglect your family, can you be trusted to remain loyal to them? They test your self-respect, your common sense and a great many faults and virtues until they know you as well as they know themselves.

Remember: you are in command here! You are in charge! You are responsible for what you choose to do. They cannot interfere with your free will, but they can certainly bend it with the tricks of their trade. Be alert. If you are so awe struck that you can't say "No!" in the beginning, build up your strength and courage. You are going to need it.

Their ridiculous demands are tests, tests, tests. You can refuse without harm, but if you refuse to do anything you will miss out on a stupendous adventure. Learn to walk the straight and narrow!

Once in the early beginnings they asked me, "Do you see that tool on the counter beside you?"

(All the time they have been telling me they could see through my eyes and hear through my ears. How could this be? Implants? They have tried to make me think so.)

This day I was in my antique shop. I looked and said, "No." I could not see anything on the counter I would classify as a tool.

"That thing with two prongs and a handle."

"Oh, that is a carving fork."

"Plunge it into your chest."

"I will not! Do you think I'm crazy?" I shouted with great vehemence.

"All right! All right! It was just a test. Forget it!"

Throughout their voluminous tests keep both feet very flat on the ground. Use superb common sense; the command module is your own noodle. Even tell them to go to hell if they get too pushy. I have done so a hundred dozen times and we are still friends, good friends, excellent friends.

Back to specifics. About the baptism:

In Betty Andreasson's initiation she was told to shower in a contrivance, but it seemed to be light instead of water. What she perceived as light was in reality a shower of energy, a revitalization or renewal of her own vital energies. Each year in days of old a Pharaoh would go through a revitalization of his vital energies in a ritual called Sed.

A number of contactees have told me of their own experience of baptism, but I know my own in best detail, so I beg your indulgence to allow me to cite that.

The SB in contact at that time (1968) kept grilling me question-and-answer style, then telling me to make a vow, then to ask for something, and finishing with the instruction "Go take a bath." That seemed a little silly, but dutifully I did as I was told.

Questions, answers, vows and baths increased until once I was told for the fifth time that day to "go take a bath." That time I protested.

"This is just too ridiculous. I'm trying to be a good sport and go along with this thing as much as possible, but five baths in one day, even quickies, is completely and absolutely absurd. Go take a flying leap in the river yourself!"

At this time I was still using the pendulum to spell out messages. Now it stopped dead for a few moments, then the pendulum spelled out, "Do you really hate us that much?" (The use of a pendulum will be described later.)

I apologized, they apologized, and that was the end of the baths, which I now realize were a form of baptism. I had made a vow and was being "washed clean."

A little while before your baptism scene will come a tutor, teacher, guide, instructor, chum, pest, rascal or friend. He will become what you insist on making of him, but he will stick like glue. A thousand times you will shout, "Get the hell out of my life!" A dozen times he will say, "Goodbye, goodbye," only to turn up again the next day as effervescent as ever. You might as well try to get rid of dandruff. He sticks.

But some wonderful adventures await in his company once you come to terms with each other. Let him know exactly how far he may intrude on your privacy. Then try to trust him if you can. Threaten to sic Jesus on him if he doesn't behave. If he thinks you are going to turn away from him into some religious haven, he will come to terms you can accept.

Now take a second look at the picture Julie has given us at the beginning of this chapter. This tutor wears an elaborate mask. In primitive societies tutors or instructors often wore masks, as they were meant to represent the "mythical ancestors."

In the 1950s contactees several times reported aliens wearing masks or partial masks. Since many contactees of that era have been severely discounted I will not mention names.

There is an old saying, "Don't throw out the baby with the bath water." I am afraid in some instances we have thrown out the baby and kept the bath water. Eventually we may find it wise to come back and reinstate some of the "babies" we threw out.

Today here in the United States, we see masks and mythical ancestors in the Kachina dancers of the Hopi Indians. Small Kachina effigies (I will not call them dolls) are given as instructional devices to the Hopi children. I refuse to call the dancers "gods", and I refuse to call the portrayal "traditions." We have effigies, mythical ancestors and dynamic representations of the purpose of life.

The instructor or mentor unquestionably will give you a hard time. In return you will travel to places you never dreamed possible to go. You will discover and photograph, draw, sketch, or write about what has become the most exciting subject in the world to you. All the while you will wonder what it really means but know it is leading to something valuable to make known.

You will meet charming and knowledgeable people you other-wise would have missed! Clues will come together in one wonderful synchronous event that will leave you gasping at the revelation...each to his own way, his own time—as long as you conscientiously do your best. It doesn't hurt to have your head a little in the clouds as long as both feet are firmly on the ground. It helps you to grow a lit-tle.

Incidentally, leave the drug scene alone. It won't help or has-ten your progress. Your instructor or tutor or mentor will take the place of any psychedelics. He can control the turnoffs and turn-ons precisely as needed. There will be no chance for slips, accidents or horror trips. He can put you through enough with his psychic tricks; you cannot take more than he is able to provide; and he guides you solicitously through the dangers. It may not seem like it while you are going, but once you have gotten through you will begin to under-stand.

Drugs, like an Ouija board, should be clinical tools, not play-things. Experience speaks. I made the mistake of playing self-made games with the pendulum and an alphabet which gave me exact messages but also hypnotized me while watching the pendulum so closely. This left the door wide open for interference and mischief from other psychic existences who did not have my best interests at heart and ended in grim disaster.

After that I went out of touch with all psychic activities for nine years until I was emotionally ready to resume contact with my former comrades. In 1977 the mental telepathic communications began and continue to this day. I eventually acquired a single mentor and have been under his tutelage for nearly 15 years. We have had some knock-down, drag-out fights, but making up has been so pleasant, each trying to outdo the other with apologies and self-blame, swearing again undying allegiance—at least one hundred and fifty times! And Hweig is his name. (Pronounced Hw-eye-jsh.)

Questions

These questions are devised particularly for those contactees who believe they are hearing voices or are having mental telepathic experiences.

1.   Why do you believe these voices or the inner communication are from UFO sources, and why do you believe they have chosen you?

2.   What incidents, events or circumstances led up to the hearing of the voices? Did you begin the incident in some manner, or was it forced or seemingly impelled on you?

3.   Did you object to the coming of the communication, and if so, how strongly?

4.   Do you feel chosen, honored or pleased that the voices are there?

5.   Was there any objection voiced against your informing others of these events at any time? If so, was this objection changed later? Relate the trend of this change in detail.

6.   Did you make any conditions under which you would receive this communication? If not, why not?

7.   What is your final verdict as to the origin of the communication and to the manner in which you receive it?

8.   Do you feel that you're being mind-invaded, mind-dominated or mind-controlled?

9.   If you could be positive as to the source of this communication and knew that the reason for it was valid and beneficial, would you cheerfully collaborate with it?

10.   In how many different ways has communication been carried on? Describe the manner in which each was imposed and approximately the time each continued. Start at the first.

11.   What was your major reaction the first time you were told you were in contact with UFO personalities?

12.   Was there a change in either mental or emotional reaction as the event continued?

13.   What was your ultimate decision mentally and emotionally? If you have made no decision, what is your present status?

14.   What value do you feel you have derived personally from this mental contact?

15.   If you had a choice, would you cut it off at once?

16. Are you able to detect in any manner the personality character-istics or traits of your communicator? Do you sometimes seem to "just know" what they are saying or doing?

17. Would you want to meet these persons?

18. Who leads the conversation, opens it, carries the most im-petus or asks the most questions, you or the communicator?

19. Are any observations made by the communicator concerning your personal surroundings or events?

20. Has the communicator offered constructive advice for your personal welfare or happiness?

21. Summarize as well as possible the subject matter of your communications, starting at the first communication and continuing chronologically as much as possible. The type of subject matter is more important now rather than specific details.

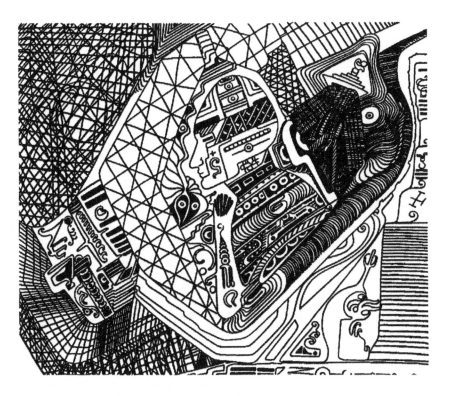

In any initiation disciplines are imposed. Here the patterns of
many intricate kinds indicate patterns of belief / knowledge
which the initiand may learn to live by.

CHAPTER SIX

Disciplines, Ordeals, and Vows

Ridicule is one of the ordeals through which the initiand must pass. It is one of the most cutting and can inflict severe pain, as most of you know too well. Make peace within yourself. You know and I know that what we tell is what we have experienced, as well as we can speak it. In what way it was the truth we do not know, but maybe we can find a reason for the experience, and by finding a reason, come to some peace within ourselves that will permit us to endure and to look with a trace of sympathy upon those who ridicule us.

Those who have not experienced cannot know. They ridicule us mostly from fear of examining the unknown too closely. Fear and perhaps a small bit of envy prompt the ridicule.

Perhaps as you hold your head in your hands and say, "Why me?" they are saying "Why not me?" Why have you been favored with this experience and not they?

"Be at peace." So many times this has been whispered to me in the night. "There is a reason for everything."

The best way I can think of here to expose some of those reasons is to allow one of those SBs to speak for them:

"We cannot judge entirely beforehand how any contactee will respond to our approaches, therefore tentative and elusive contacts of different kinds must be made previous to a big, open, vital contact. Sometimes years are spent in this getting-acquainted routine before we dare expose ourselves in an open confrontation.

"Many hours are spent in analyzing, planning, judging, and re-planning, changing our tactics constantly as necessity demands. The major portion of our planning time is spent in evaluating the particular and specific pattern of beliefs that the developing individual seems loathe to abandon as he matures.

"Many beliefs of the younger years are abandoned along the way, along with the belief in Santa Claus, Easter Bunny, fairies and the infallibility of parents. Others persist to our dying day, and it is on the fabric of these beliefs that we weave our design. I use that word "design" with forethought. The essence of our design is the immutability of the human ego to self-recrimination. An overstuffed sentence? All right, let us say no one wants to take the blame for something he can legitimately assign to someone else. It is a matter of ego preservation and self-pride, indeed, of self-respect.

"Therefore we build our design around this particular person's belief in his own worth. It is amazing how many people have little confidence in their own value. Their self-esteem has been squashed by life events at an early age, and their response to our tickling of their ego is a groan of self-distrust.

"Our first task is to put our contactee through a series of self-experiences that allows him to see himself as a worthy person potential of prideful accomplishments and gratifying attainments.

"Through our manipulations, which we may describe later, we persuade him to run over in his mind all the mistakes and errors of his past. He finds himself picking through these painful memories and examining them thoroughly, one by one, in the light of his later years. A kind of mental catharsis takes place, relieving him of his self-condemnation and profound regret for events past that he felt should have been better handled. He comes to see he has not been all that bad or wicked or sinful or gauche.

"Now he can forgive himself, forget the incidents, and go on with great relief from anxiety and stress, with buoyant good humor, a bounce in his step, and a sparkle in his eye. This catharsis from self-recrimination may take years, but it is the first and necessary step to bring his pattern of beliefs into a workable arrangement with our plans for him.

"Our second step is to give him an opportunity to learn, to extend his knowledge of many things, places and peoples, to fill in his educational background, not by going to school, but by travel, new experiences, exposure to new ideas and contact with different strata of people. Here there will be considerable sloughing off of old ideas and beliefs and a tentative trying on of new. If he proves obstinate to change, we leave him; there are many other potential contactees to be tested and trained.

If his mind be agile and receptive, we continue to find him new adventures; all the time we are analyzing his present and planning his future, preparing a scenario, a drama in which he will have a leading role. We plant along the way many mysteries that will only "make sense" or "add up" when he has reached a certain point of sophistication and understanding. These are like clues in a detective story. Only much later will their purpose, use, value and meaning be understood.

"An example of these mysteries may be that we want him to read a certain type of book. We manipulate his path so that he stumbles over certain books, which he feels "inspired" to take up and read. Or we make sure that he is in a specific place to meet a person he had no thought or intention of meeting. Or he finds himself *not* doing something he had fervently intended to do. At the last instant he says, "Oh to heck with it," and lets the opportunity go by. Or he may find himself rushing off to a particular place without having made the slightest plan to do so, and asking himself bewilderedly, 'What am I doing here? What am I doing this for?'

"Because we impelled or inspired him to do so by means of several manipulations we are capable of using.

"Thus we put him into new activities, new adventures, new contacts and exposure to new ideas, from which arise his opportunities to change and expand his pattern of beliefs.

"We maneuver, manipulate and expose him to the forces of change in every way we can, but never to the point of smothering or obstructing his free will. He chooses according to what he is and what he will be.

"And we plant seemingly insignificant factors in his life that will be essential to something very important in his future. Thus we begin to find and tie together all the threads that will weave the fabric of his refined basic beliefs.

"After our contactee is well on the way to forgiving himself for all his supposed crimes, misdemeanors and silly mistakes and has begun to revalue his basic beliefs, we begin to work on his dependence on others. This is an even tougher battle, for life has taught him more about his weaknesses than his strengths and has led him to lean heavily or lightly on the broad shoulder and strong back of some figure, more or less heroic to him, to whom he gives allegiance, and too often, his own strength. To wean him from that dependency and to bring him to rely upon his own strength is a most difficult and wearying task. Therefore he is led to many events that expose him to himself to make him aware of what he is, and more important, of what he can be. Always the choice is his—his free will is not hindered—but he is made aware, through experience, by passing through events, not by preaching. Some of the events, indeed many, are hurtful, not because we wish to be mean, but because we wish a change to take place. Preaching can never produce the change that experience can.

"We must help him to find not only strength in himself, but confidence to go ahead without advice or overt directions to produce the results that he desires.

"Erasing fears means changing his beliefs and finding new beliefs that bring out self-confidence, as his self-catharsis produced self-respect.

"Believing now in himself more than in the advisability of dependence on others, he has matured into a person whom we can use and whom we can inspire with beliefs that will make him available to our purpose. But only if those beliefs are compatible to what he has always been and what he is. We do not force him in any way to be untrue to his principles, his values or his integrity. We want collaboration of the highest moral caliber, of compassion and of common sense. Formal education is not a presiding factor, though we try to introduce him to wider horizons and expanded views.

"If a contactee becomes obverse to these qualities, if his ego super-inflates, if he goes sky rocketing off in alternate directions, we drop him. Thud! That's right, we drop him. Frequently then he will come to a dead end or a sudden stop in his headlong flight. If he can recognize his error, re-evaluate himself, turn back into the way of practicality and human worth, we mentally pick him up again and try as persuasively as we can, without damaging either his self-esteem or his free will, to allow him to pick up the previous course he had once followed, the course of responsible endeavor.

"Those contactees who elevate themselves without true reason and find themselves unable to come down from their ego fling are left right there, babbling forever about past glories and advancing not one step further in the direction of human evolution or collaborating with the cosmic forces and principles that guide them as well as ourselves. They are left to flutter helplessly in the breeze of their own blasts of noncomprehension. Such persons give a bad reputation to the whole course of UFO-Contactee experiences. Unfortunately the most comprehending and best evolving contactees are usually the most quiet and unobtrusive. The bombastic rhetoric of the "fallen angels" obscures and distorts the calm exploration and valuable observations of the staid and steady.

"Once our contactee has reached self-esteem and self-dependency, we can hope to bolster his self-assurance. This means he becomes convinced of the rightness of his activities, his choice, his path, his responsibilities and his duties. Becoming definitely convinced of these, he can now march firmly forward into collaboration with us, giving of his best potentials and re-affirming his faith in himself at every step.

"There remains one further step; and that is to free himself of all that would hinder his march to his own destiny. He must not abandon his task for the sake of some clinging demand from others. He must become wise as well as patient to consider and reconsider what is necessary and advantageous to his course, and what is confining, obscuring or hindering. Some of his most cherished and basic beliefs must be re-examined from the view of his "new" self. Some of his strongest ties must be loosened. This does not mean abandoning family, friends or social responsibilities. It means careful measuring of time and talents to give each its just and honorable due, but no more; no sacrificing of one to the other, simply a re-weighing, re-measuring, re-adjusting, a budgeting of time and purposes. This is the most difficult of all his assignments, but it must be thoroughly done before he can step out confidently and surely upon the path we have selected for him, and which, in the long run, he has chosen for himself."

So the SBs have spoken and explained their "reasons for everything" concerning the disciplines, ordeals and troubles they put us through. I could not have begun to explain it so well, though I have lived through and experienced the evidence of it all.

In my own experiences, my most abject fear was that I was about to be taken over by some alien personality! That I would be "lost" to my former life that I would change abruptly into someone else. Actually, I sort of liked myself as I was, and although I knew I had to advance in many ways and to clean up my act, so to speak, I did not want to lose sight of myself or allow someone else to take over. I felt that I, as I was, had some kind of duty to perform in the world and that was why I was here. Not some noble mission or exotic purpose, just some humble duty that had to be done and which I had come to do and which I jolly well intended to do, as soon as I could find out what it was! One of the most horrible night experiences had to do with this theme.

On this night, in 1968, I was awakened and scared senseless by the feeling that someone was drawing a sheathlike material through my body as though it were another skin being drawn between the outer skin and the flesh. I could feel it coming up over my knees, thighs, abdomen and chest, rapidly being drawn upward. I sensed several presences on either side of me working hard to draw it further and further. I got the panicky notion that once it was drawn up over my face, I would be someone else, I would no longer be me.

I struggled and fought, trying to move, but unable to do so; the sheath was drawn inexorably up. I sent out every mental cry of anguish I could devise, but I could not cry out vocally. I was paralyzed, unable to move a muscle or make a sound. Up to my neck it came; it touched my chin. With a terrible effort, I flung myself sideways and cried, "Oh God help! Help me! Help me!"

Then the presences were gone. There was no movement of any kind near my bed. A nightmare? Wait. Just a second.

My body relaxed and I could sit up. Then there was a sensation of a red light being shown around the room, just under the ceiling. Around and around it went on the side walls, crisscrossing over my body. Each time there was a terrible burning sensation. Then through the night a whisper came, "This is our laser beam!" Even in that state I wondered, "Beam, I thought it was laser ray." But they whispered again, "Laser beam." And I realized the whisper was in my ear, a definite vibration of sound, just as though someone were whispering in my ear. It was altogether different from the former telepathy which had been just a movement of meanings, or words. This was an actual vibration of a physical sound.

"It burns," I moaned. "It bums." And I lay gasping with fear until presently I fell asleep.

I do not know myself how to analyze these experiences to make any sense. I just know they were not dreams, they were something very real.

But what was the purpose? To make me think? To make me aware? More testing in their own aggravating fashion? They could have been induced illusions, induced dreams, but still in essence very, very real. I would not try to fathom them on the basis of totally physical reality, but I would like to know what they were meant to convey, what idea lay behind them. What was I supposed to learn, or remember?

It is such events as this that are so hard for each contactee to accept and to try to understand. But it is such events as this that we must realize are not hallucinations of our own making; they are psychic events imposed upon us. That much understanding will relieve us of the fear that we have gone completely out of our mind. Accepting them as induced events will allow us to evaluate them on the basis of their intended meaning. There are still many puzzles to solve here.

I am sure the experiences of that night were not ordeals just for the sake of ordeals; they had a further purpose that I have not defined.

Another event I have not been able to fathom was certainly an induced illusion. I was lying in bed reading. I glanced down and thought I caught a glimpse of a heavy cord being drawn across my arm. It was white and, surprisingly, square! I could see it being pulled across my arm but could see nothing that was pulling it. There was a cold moist sensation where it touched. That, too, has never been explained.

I have mentioned that I made various vows during this time, most of which I cannot remember now, but which I am told my subconscious remembers and has obeyed. I also had to vow to keep each one of these a secret. I must have done that, since I can't remember them myself! But the making of vows went on for weeks even after telepathy was established.

Every time I made a vow to keep a secret, the pendulum would spell out, "Ask for something." I still used it as a backup to the telepathy.

I thought and thought but could not come up with anything that seemed appropriate. I certainly did not intend to be "bought off" in exchange for the vows, not by someone or something I knew nothing about. So each time I would say, "Whatever you want to give."

But as I thought it over one day I decided, "There is something those fellows could do for me." So the next time they said "Ask for something," I said, "I want to see the insides of a UFO."

There was no immediate response. But one night I awoke after an early sleep to sense several presences in my room. I could not actually see them, but I sensed that there were several very tall men and one very short woman. Later I learned they called her Myra, and she was a kind of doctor whom they had on hand in case there were any mishaps.

One of the tall men pressed close to my bed, or at least his telepathic "voice" seemed to come from quite close.

"In response to your request, we are going to take you to see the inside of a UFO. Are you ready?"

"Yes." I was ready. In those days I always wore a long calico granny gown instead of a nightgown, as I never knew what was going to show up in my bedroom at night.

An instant later I was standing on a platform with guard rails. It extended out into a vast cylinder.

Below the narrow platform was deep dark space and I clung to the rail, as I have a fear of heights, or in this case, depths. Above me the cylinder stretched many feet skyward. Something whirled around the top, and above I could see the stars. The cylinder grew lighter as it rose to the top, and it seemed to be a whitish silver metal. Across on the other side and a little lower down I could see another platform and three men in blue coveralls worked in a bluish light. When one opened a small door in the panel before them I could see blue darting flames like lightning and I got the idea of an energy control panel.

If it had not been so dark on the platform, I probably could have seen the men who accompanied me, as we were all now in the same state, perhaps out-of-body state, but they were just forms in the darkness.

Someone opened the door leading to the platform and stood outlined in the yellow light from a hallway. He said two curt words, which for some reason I remember as "That's enough." The men and I turned to walk through the door but instantly I was back in bed again. The tall person leaning over me said, "You wanted to see the inside of a UFO. Now you have done so."

For years I was miffed. Finally, I mentioned it to my communicator.

"Why did you fellows play that joke on me when you took me to see the inside of a UFO?"

"Joke? There wasn't any joke. We did just what you asked."

"You knew perfectly well I wanted to see things like your desks and bookcases and beds and pillows and the kitchen sink and curtains. I didn't want to see that dam cylinder."

He laughed so long that I was beginning to get mad all over again.

"Oh my dear woman," he said. "Of course that was what you wanted to see! But we, being men, showed you what a man would have wanted to see, the mechanisms and energy controls. We have been a bit peeved at you. You seemed so inappreciative of our very great efforts to get you there!"

He added, "Now you see why we prefer pictorial telepathy to communicate rather than words. If you had given us any kind of picture in your mind we could not have made such a mistake. Verbal communication can lead to many such misunderstandings."

Well, at least that is something explained!

One of the most difficult questions we contactees try to answer is how to categorize our various experiences. While it is not a life-and-death matter that we are able to do so, it does make us feel better to be able to tie some kind of label on the event.

Categories of Experiences

1. Dreams and dream-like events
2. Excursions
   a.   mind travel
   b.   out-of-body experience
   c.   semi-corporeal events

The first category is dreams and dream-like events. We are never sure whether the dream is reminding us of an actual (physical) occurrence or whether it is an induced dream trying to get a message across without a physical counterpart.

Either way, a dream is a dream, and its symbols can be interpreted as in any other dream, based again on what those particular symbols encountered mean to that participant.

Sometimes I am sure those SBs are most avid students of Dr. Carl G. Jung, their antics so fit into his various expositions and theories of human behavior. I believe they must have used his work as a basis in their planning, hoping maybe that we would recognize this and use it as a way of interpretation and understanding.

If it is convenient, by all means read *Man and His Symbols* by Jung and his colleagues. It is written in non-technical terms, so even I can understand most of it.

The second category might be those excursions when they come, particularly at night, and take us somewhere. Of course we do not go in physical body. We note that the transitions are too abrupt. These can be mind travel excursions, out-of body-experiences or semi-corporeal events. There may be other kinds of ways to accompany them, but I do not know of them. In any of these three states we find ourselves abruptly there. There is no transition of going out of doors, getting into a car and driving to a rendezvous. We are first in bed, or wherever, and then—just there. Trying to separate these three states is difficult.

In mind travel you view a scene as though it were on a wrap-around screen. There is no sound of footsteps or other sounds, no odors, no tactile sense, which is perhaps the most telling clue. You have left everything at home except your power of sight and vision. You only observe and react to the observation.

In the out-of-body state you have a much greater range of sensory experience. You can hear voices, feel what you were walking on, take hold of something but not to manipulate it. You cannot pick something off the floor, for example.

In the semi-corporeal state you can do almost anything you could as fully corporeal, but not to the same degree. You can pick up a normal physical object and even replace it on a table, but only with the severest of concentration, and then with many fumbles. In a non-concentrated state your hand and the object would by-pass each other. One needs to be psychically adept, or to be in company with such, in order to use the semi-corporeal state in a fairly normal corporeal way, and even then usually several persons concentrating together are needed to ensure firm control. In the story of Betty Andreasson, Quazgaa and his three clones concentrating together made it possible for her to proceed in a fairly normal manner.

I first took my own experience in visiting the cylinder to be mind travel, but on contemplation, I realized I could not then have grasped the railing, nor felt myself walking on the platform, nor heard the man in the doorway speak. I had to be in a semi-corporeal experience under the control of the several men who accompanied me. Or it might have been an out-of-body experience, which would have been just my psychic essence present. I cannot define this more closely now.

These several types of experiences cannot be interpreted entirely through symbols as we do with dreams. There are symbols within the experiences that may be interpreted as dreams, but part of the observation is actual and must be interpreted as physical facts. The cylinder was a fact, something for the physical data man to study. The men working with the blue flames were symbols of energy controllers; I am sure that the observation was pure illusion.

It is almost impossible to decide how much is physical and how much is imposed psychic event. No matter how we categorize or define them for our own peace of mind, the final interpretation is based the same, on the psychological impact on the contactee, something carefully chosen for his own unique participation.

However we categorize the event, mind travel, or out-of- body experience (OBE) or semi-corporeal, the main emphasis for us is that the event was real in some condition of reality. The category only tells us how the event was imposed. Far more important is the impact on the contactee and his interpretation of the event. This tells us why, or the meaning behind the scene.

I am sure those SBs have an awful lot of fun cooking up some of those scenes, such as having a contactee run headlong into an asparagus man, or having a ball game with Bigfoot! I can just see them slapping their knees and guffawing as they plan.

They do not -- repeat _not_ -- always mean what they say. I was told many times, "Be wary. Look under the words." Obviously I was not to take what was said at face value always. What value then was I supposed to give it?

Remember the Frenchman who was challenged when he gave the correct time?

"You lie! It is four o'clock!"

If he had been told to think about time, he would have said, "Oui! Oui!" and, not understanding, promptly forgotten all about it. The challenge was an attention getter.

Like the man who trained mules said, the first rule was to hit the mule over the head with a 2 X 4 to get his attention. The challenge, "You lie!" was the verbal 2 X 4 . Probably the Frenchman is still thinking about time many years later!

Questions

1. Have you been instructed or felt impelled to:

   Diet?

   Observe better health habits?

   Organize time better?

   Be more practical with money?

   Take better care of possessions?

   Take trips to research centers?

   Be more observant of others?

   Participate in environmental activities?

   Take part in wildlife preservation?

   Restructure your basic beliefs?

2. Have you been able to handle ridicule? How?

3. Were you led to certain studies or learning processes? More about this in next chapter.

4. Were you led or somehow coerced into unexpected travels? Where? For what purpose?

5. Have you met new people or had new experiences of a type you always wanted to but never expected to? Relate in some detail.

6. Have you found yourself going somewhere unexpectedly or doing something you had not planned?

7. Have you felt as a result of your experiences that you have more self-esteem, more self-assurance, more self-dependence than formerly?

8. How have you readjusted and budgeted your time and purposes between alternate responsibilities?

9. Do you remember making any formal vows? Describe them, if you are not forbidden.

   For the next questions, relate the experiences fully, even though you cannot positively identify which category they belong to.

10. Have you had any experience that you identify as out-of- body?

    Mind travel?

    A semicorporeal state?

11. Relate any specific ordeals as fully as you like.

12. Relate any induced dreams. Interpret any symbols that you believe were specifically designed for you.

The creeds, customs, traditions of the life an initiand is to lead must be thoroughly learned. To the left above are symbols that look like bits of heraldry but not exactly so we are to think of the ideas that heraldry represents the ideas of old families treasuring certain virtues and passing on that tradition.

CHAPTER SEVEN

Traditions:

Cultural, Moral, Spiritual

All initiates study the spiritual traditions and moral evaluations of their own people, but to a contactee this means worldwide and from the beginning: research into cultural, moral and spiritual traditions.

Perhaps it will be clearer if we put this into a formal listing. Learning the traditions has always meant learning about:

1. Creation of the world
2. Creation of humanity
3. The primal cause
4. God and the Creative Ones
5. Heroes of old
6. Ancient ones who formulated moral and social laws
7. Relationships between humans and animals
8. Relationships between humans and nature/nature spirits

In the initiation of contacteeship you will find yourself studying, researching and traveling to places of archaeological and anthropological significance and learning about such peoples as the Sumerians, Babylonians, Akkadians, Assyrians, the earliest Egyptians, Pre-Incas, Incas, Mayans, Aztecs and their neighbors, Hopis, and the mound builders of the Midwest

You will be surprised to find in how many ways these various people and places fit together. Each student will derive his own understanding and concentrate on his own particular area of interest, his own "piece of the puzzle."

Another area of study for those who do not particularly take to the study of the ancient civilizations might be the study of various religions and religious documents of the past: the Vedas of India, the book of Chilam Balaam of the Mayas and the Books of the Dead of Egypt or Tibet. Each contactee searches out and studies what is significant to himself.

One may concentrate his major study in the mythologies of the past or such subjects as fairies, leprechauns, nature spirits, dryads, nymphs or the great God Pan. Another may choose American Indian studies, their legends and myths or what cultural anthropology can tell them. The Indian studies bear heavily on Man and his relationships to animals and to nature. Another may choose excursions into psychic studies, but I hope he has a guide along, for the way is dangerous to the uninitiated and unguided. Whatever the course of study chosen, each contactee will choose for himself what feels to be peculiarly his own.

If you have mental contact you may receive explicit instructions to go to a certain place and do definite things. My first instruction was to go to the Edgar Cayce library at Virginia Beach and get all the material available on Atlantis, and next to go to the Smithsonian and get material on Sumeria.

Or you may just have an overwhelming urge or impulse to go to a certain place to investigate certain aspects. One contactee has been telling me about her overwhelming desire to go to Maya country to photograph and study what she could. During her experiences there she had a time loss, became ill and was worried about a possible contact with radiation. She was slated for a hypnosis session, and then declared "I am going back!" She has more courage than I!

Another contactee and dear friend has spent years studying earth changes, volcanoes and earthquakes. Recently, her interest has turned to Indians, the Hopis in particular, and she has undertaken a quest that can only be called spiritual in relation to them.

I have been pushed to study symbols, codes and epigraphy, and I have recently worked on several puzzles, codes and messages written in very old languages, with some success in deciphering, but not perfectly. I feel this is practice work, and I am waiting for something really exciting to come along.

I was told my task was "interpreting," and when I asked what, the answer was, "It will come or be sent to you."

One element of initiation that I have been expecting but have not found in a complete sense is that initiates are taught a secret language, code or passwords. I did have an experience with what was apparently a kind of password.

One warm summer evening in 1968, I was reading, and I had the front door open in my little "chicken coop," as my husband-to-be had called it. I was living alone at the time. It was quite dark, so I did not see the man coming to my door until he knocked, and I went to the open door. He stood back from the light so I could not see him very closely, but he seemed rather slight of build, well dressed and professional looking.

He said he had come to meet his son there, and he gave me his son's name. I said I was sorry that I had never heard that name. He must have the wrong address; maybe he wanted 8th Street, this was 8th Avenue.

"No, this is the place," he said, "my son described it perfectly, a small house behind a larger house, and the driveway came in just like this."

"I'm really sorry, but this is not the place. Does your son have a phone? You could come in and call him."

He insisted that this was the place that had been described, but he would not bother me by coming in. He had seen a phone booth up the street, and he would go there. I thought that a bit silly when the phone was right inside the door.

He seemed to hesitate and made some conversation. I got the idea that I had to tell him something. I really panicked, thinking he would leave before I could tell him what I had to say; only I didn't know what it was.

He drew a paper out of his pocket and read this astonishing statement,

"The Way of Man has been limited by his lack of knowledge of himself. Let Man study his own soul if he would save the world. All is revealed within to one who searches. The time will come when true freedom, freedom of the spirit, will be known on this earth."

I knew then what I had to tell him. It was a line from some writing I had done several years before. I blurted it out very clumsily, "Before the year 2000, men are going to have to learn how to use a new force coming into their lives, or they will destroy themselves."

I had envisioned this as a kind of psychic and/or spiritual force. I was not sure which.

He simply said, "Good night," and he stepped off the porch.

I reached for the door, intending to close it, and when I glanced up a second later, he was gone. I did not see how he could have gone around the corner of the house in front so quickly. He just dissolved into the night.

Much, much later I was told that my sentence was the password to verify myself as a person they had been told to find. The man was in a semi-corporeal state, which was why he would not enter the house or come too fully into the light. He was afraid by some accident that I might discover something strange in his being. He was the one with whom I had mental contact later and who called himself Jamie.

Betty Andreasson once began to speak in a strange language. Her story contains all the major factors of a perfect initiation.

Any number of contactees have been given alphabets and vocabularies in what are purported to be languages from other planets. I collect all of these that I can, as well as any messages written in symbols. A few make some kind of sense, but I have not derived much benefit from most of them, due to my own lack of understanding, I am sure. I am hoping to improve!

In the more primitive societies, much time is spent learning traditional songs, chants and dances and going through various rituals. These are not too evident in the contactee initiation, though some events may border on the ritualistic.

One night in my little "chicken coop" I was impelled to go through a series of ritualistic gestures. I did not hear a word of command, but I was obeying something unspoken. I was in a kind of trance.

First, I laid aside everything I wore, even my glasses (which I take off only to sleep). I later decided that this was a gesture to indicate the laying aside of all worldly possessions. Then kneeling, I made a strange gesture with both arms curved over my head, something like the horns of Hathor. Then I dropped my hands to my thighs and rested a moment.

Again I raised them both skyward as though supplicating, and in an incredibly graceful (for me) movement slowly lowered them sinuously to my sides as though I were indicating falling rain or a shower of something. My arms bent at the elbow, and I raised my hands, cupped together a little above eye level, receiving bounty. As the hands seemingly filled, they dropped lower and lower with the weight of that received. After a moment's pause, I lifted them again, still cupped, and turning them over began to scatter the bountiful gifts, moving my hands back and forth over the world. I knew I was making a pledge to share whatever I might receive with the whole world.

I had heard no voice, and nothing was spoken. I do not know how I came to follow this ritual, or how I was "told" what to do. But I knew what I had promised.

Questions

1.   Have you been told or felt impelled to go to certain places for research and study? If so, where and for what purpose?

2.   Have you been told or felt compelled to study ancient civilizations? If so, which ones?

3.   Have you been led to study world religions? If so, which ones?

4.   Have you been led to study metaphysical subjects? Describe your studies.

5.   Have you spent much time studying mythologies? If so, which ones?

6.   Have you felt a closeness to and desire to study about Indians? If so, which ones and in what aspects?

7.   Have you been told or felt compelled to go to certain places? If so, where?

8.   Have you been told or felt compelled to study psychic phenomena? Describe.

9.   Describe any other compulsions or directions to traditional areas of study.

10.   What do you feel you have learned or derived benefit from in your studies? Please describe in detail.

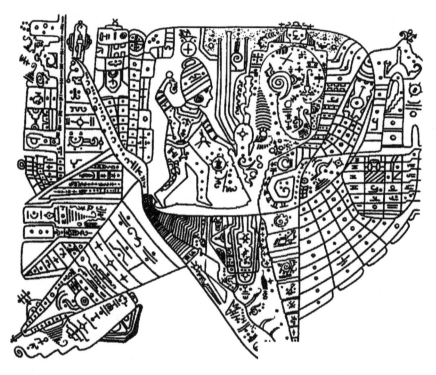

Tasks of ever increasing difficulty are imposed In this picture the woman seems to be working on the insides of a human head. (I am sure this is meant figuratively!) Her wrench is peculiarly shaped for such a strange enterprise. She seems to be reconstructing the headful of ideas and thinking abilities, perhaps adding new mental capacities. On the right is the torso from which the head was taken, temporarily. The voluminous sleeves of the torso are also the collar descending from the neck. The torso sprouts a bit of new growth vegetation indicating the two parts will be re-attached as soon as the head is reconstructed.

CHAPTER EIGHT

Tasks

When we come to the subject of the larger tasks each contactee undertakes as his rightful domain, we come to so many divergent paths that it is almost impossible to state a course that all have, or all will, follow. Since the UFO phenomenon is worldwide, so too are the courses that a contactee may follow, each in his own way, each on his own timing. All, however, find their tasks ever increasing in difficulty, as did Hercules, Gilgamesh or Hiawatha, each feeling a sense of climbing to some apex of potential.

Contactees are men and women existing in the world around them in places like China, Norway, Australia, Brazil and the United States. The tasks that they are given and have adopted for their own are in total harmony to their own time and place. So vast a multitude of varying tasks cannot be encapsulated in a single diagram.

The insistence that contactees study the cultures and religions of ancient civilization, as well as current ones, is not to make us take any specific doctrine to ourselves, but to show us the diversity and sometimes the similarities among them all, to move us out of the narrow and provincial spheres where we were and to move us into a worldwide, deep comprehension of the ways and thoughts of humanity.

Some will find their larger tasks in creative endeavor, in writing, drawing, painting, photography, in areas of scientific research, in following ideas of their own invention, or in pursuing uses for the latest technological advancements. At this time, for example, the entire future of laser technology has not even been dreamed.

The sudden increase in such technological advancements, in the uses of lasers, in space travel, and in use of nuclear energies has brought us to a split in our course of civilization as impactive and disastrous as the leap from the nomadic hunter-gatherer culture to the ways of settlement brought about through the advancement of agriculture.

I can well imagine that it was the women who started all this, bringing about the trauma of the mighty hunter as he was reduced to the unglorified role of the planter or harvester. Women grew tired of tramping in the wake of their hirsute mates with the provisions, sleeping skins and a kid or two on their bowed backs (and probably another in their bellies), while the hunter kept his hands free to hurl a spear or wield a knife.

One day the women held a kaffee klatch and decided among themselves that enough was enough. "We're gonna civilize these brutes," they agreed. When the lusty hunters readied for another hunt they found themselves faced with an ultimatum.

"We stay here!" said the matrons. "Good place here. Food on trees. Fish in water. We build caves on top ground, good poles here, mud, good thatch. Cool when hot sun. Warm when cold winds. Dry when water falls. Our kids no get sick, die so much. We put seeds, bulbs, bush in ground. Stay here alia time. Pick seeds." The men found arguments, perhaps even beatings, useless.

"You go hunt, trap, fish," said the gals. "You come home, food fixed for you right now. You eat all day, make babies all night. We go on hunt no more forever."

It was a telling argument. The men accepted the treaty. Until the first harvest.

"Come," said the women. "The seed stalks bend. The hail comes. We all hurry, hurry. We need everybody. You come." The men demurred. They were mighty hunters. They would not demean themselves to do a woman's work.

"You help or else," cried the ladies. "We no fix food. We no make babies. You come." They went. They became harvesters, planters and then farmers. But it was a traumatic change. He who had dressed in the magnificent leopard's skin now wore a cloak of plaited reeds. It kept off the rain, but it scratched. It was an embarrassment. Where had the glory gone?

It must have taken the embarrassed hunters two or three or even more generations to subdue their pride and become willing farmers. The first groupings of mud and thatch huts became villages. A man with too much grain learned to barter with another who had too much pig. Civilization had come, but where was the pride? Where was the glory?

When one stays in one place, one acquires possessions. (And how!)

"This is mine, that is yours, and mine is more than yours."

"My woman paints the sun wheel in red ochre on my plaited cloak. My cloak is more powerful medicine than yours."

A new kind of pride and glory emerged, but it took generations to evolve, to become real. Where does that leave the first nomad hunters who turned to agriculture? In lost self-esteem, bitterness, resentment, and trauma, trauma, trauma all the way.

Why do I report this? Because this is exactly where the family farmers, mill workers, loggers, factory assemblers and oil drillers stand today, in precisely the same circumstances. Only the pursuits are different. And trauma all the way!

We can see on every side the changes in our agricultural- economic-industrial age, and the ruptures in the lives of those so engaged as we leap across the chasm to the age of technological wonders.

The vital tasks that the contactees have been coerced, guided or somehow induced to undertake all have reference to this traumatic change in people's lives, changes only now becoming visible on every side. More changes will come, so rapid and destructive to the old ways that we cannot now imagine them.

Our institutions, financial, social, educational and religious, will feel the impact and the necessity to change. It is a time when the lapses and misdirections of the old and present institutions will bring about an inner collapse, perpetrated by themselves, not by divine judgment. They cannot continue their makeshift and patched-up policies and flourish under the new age. New ways of observation and inspection by governments and the community at large will nullify and eradicate the techniques of evasion as heretofore practiced. This observation is only a matter of common sense. As more and more sophisticated communication devices multiply and spread across the world, so secrets and secret operations become less and less possible.

Technology has caught up and overtaken the family farm, so it will swallow up many another business and industry. More technology-geared and robotized industry means more labor disputes and more industrial employees turning to new jobs or to no job at all. Then they form groups, which soon become unguided mobs, and eventually, when an opportunist leader comes, hungry armies. When the nomad hunters turned from killing the wild animals of the woods, they turned to killing each other, found it was a far greater sport and named it *war.*

The tasks the contactees have undertaken will sooner or later lead them to be cognizant of these problems, in one degree and sense or another, and each will have his opportunity to, in some way, control the course of events, or more likely, to help alleviate the impact.

Many innocent and well-meaning people and their families will fall victim to the coming changes. The handwriting is on the wall for *all* civilization. There are truly much graver concerns in the world than Saddam Hussein.

Note again Julie Wilkinson's skillful and fantastic drawings throughout this book. Here is hard-fact evidence of what the SBs have in mind for contactees—skills practiced and learned well. Julie had no experience in art until she began drawing by automatic processes, just as many have been led to automatic writing. "At first the drawing was very primitive," said Julie, meaning it was very simple. "But after four years and hundreds and hundreds of drawings, it has become very complex." (As we can witness) "Sometimes the subject matter changes abruptly. Right now it is planes, all shapes and descriptions. The latest have looked like boomerangs."

At the same time other events are imposed upon her, vivid dreams that seem to have meaning and purpose but have not yet been analyzed. At times unwanted pressures and demands are levied on her, and she fights to escape them.

The major difficulty of contacteeship is that each must go through it alone. The meanings are unique to the individual, and no one else can adequately interpret them. One either survives or goes under by himself.

That is why this book is written, to offer a little companionship, a little fellow sympathy, for all it is worth. We cannot go through the events for other contactees, but we can let them know that we care, that we share their fears and anxieties and that we have found a way of enduring, tenuous and shaky as it is.

But should one of those SBs suddenly jump in my face shouting *"Boo!"* I guarantee to faint on the spot.

Question

Have you zeroed in on some larger task that you feel compelled to pursue, such as the study of ancient civilizations or religions, codes, symbols, scientific research or inventions? Describe as fully as possible, giving approximate dates and the course of events.

The ever-increasing tasks are like climbing a ladder. At the apex the initiand receives special revelations or a vision or even speaks with God. Here the personage receives the revelation of the new world he is about to enter. While the world seems technological it is surrounded by spiritual flames.

CHAPTER NINE

Revelations

As contactees settle in on one large task, they quickly discover that the way becomes more and more difficult, more complex, more time- (and money-) consuming until they have a definite sense of climbing up a stair, up a spiral, up a ladder, up a mountain or whatever climbing means to them. If you do not feel that you have been climbing, turn around and look behind you from whence you came!

In the primitive societies, the apex of climbing is an actual physical event after the tasks had been completed. Sometimes this is a pole, or bared tree trunk to which objects or fetishes had been attached. When the graduating initiand reaches the top, certain final secrets are revealed. Here, if he is in a trance-like state, he may believe that the gods have spoken to him and revealed sacred truths and meanings.

As the contactee reaches the peak of his endeavor, he will begin to "see the light." Things that have happened to him will begin to "make sense." He can now fit some pieces of the puzzle together, not the total UFO mysteries, but the pieces that concern himself. He will begin to understand meanings and realize purposes and see why certain things have happened and had to happen in the manner in which they have. It takes time, a lot of thought and the piecing together of many twos and twos and twos.

If he gets too close to something that is not wanted to be known yet, he may find himself-embroiled in a bit of trouble that serves to discredit him in the eyes of his associates. He must not be too clever! It is not wise to demand to know too much too soon. "Lest he become as one of us!"

No, I do not believe that gods have spoken to us at the moment of revelation. The communications we receive come through a certain group of SBs who call themselves, not surprisingly, the Communicators, but they receive directives of what they are to communicate, in a general way, from those they acknowledge to be their superiors.

Perhaps this is a good time to include the "Hierarchy" of the persons, personages, entities and psychic existences who take part in the total UFO events. This was given to me some years ago and has been revised recently to fit my more extended experience and "understanding." I am not so sure about the understanding, but the experiences I cannot deny!

What follows is all dictation by my tutor, mentor, instructor, friend, scalawag and tease, Hweig, pronounced "hw-eye-jsh."

Hierarchy of UFO Collaborators

Introducing the Communicators, in this instance: Hweig, Amorto, and Jamie. These are adopted names for communication with this particular contactee. For others we use other names.

PART I.

A.   An Earth fellowship
B.   Thought reconstructs (explained later)
   1.   Legendary ones
      a.   Nature spirits and "gods"
      b.   Fauns, leprechauns and elves
      c.   Fairies, gnomes, brownies
      d.   Centaurs, sylphs, undines, satyrs
      e.   Spirits of the air
   2.   Ancient heroes
   3.   Mythical beings

PART II.

A.   Energy Existences
   1.   Messengers
   2.   Psychic Connectives
   3.   Inspirators
B.   Instructors
C.   Space stations (mother ships)
D.   Planet X, its colonies and outposts
E.   Overlords and Confederation of Planets

F.   Guardians

G.   Creative Forces

    1.   Planners

    2.   Instigators

H.   The Source (of spiritual essence)

I.   The Radiance

    1.   Place of Being

    2.   The Power

    3.   The Active Force

PART III.

A.   Earth world

B.   Co-existent worlds

C.   Outer space—planetary

"We, Hweig, Amorto and Jamie, are all as physical and corporeal as yourselves, but we can extend ourselves into other non-corporeal or semi-corporeal selves and be cognizant of each and all simultaneously, although the various "selves" may be active in separate places, or even separate time dimensions.

"We are no more superhuman or supernormal than yourselves—you of the Earth have merely forgotten.

"We said, "We come to waken, to make aware."

And that is our purpose, for our own reasons, and our own ends as much as yours. There will be no antagonistic invasion of Earth if we can meet and discuss on levels of friendship and understanding.

"We have had contacts for many centuries with Earth, but always from our own viewpoint and for our own desires and purposes. Now we are trying to see from the Earthling's view and understanding.

"There are several manners in which we are trying to make contact with Earth at this time. In this we use telepathic contact, and we are the communicators. We are in charge of carrying out on Earth instructions received from elsewhere. Our instructions are quite broad and general; the specifics we provide according to circumstance.

"Material is sent to us to "deliver" and general instructions are given as to how to proceed with the various tests and experiments. We are the people of the UFOs, but we are not the originators of this total experiment. We carry out our instructions to the best of our abilities, and our abilities are great. Therefore, we cannot always give you the "proofs" you ask for, not until it is released for us to do so. We work for a cause larger than our own."

The Earth Fellowship

"We have mentioned the fellowship before, but we repeat it here to keep the thoughts all together. The Earth fellowship, of which we are members, and in which you are training, is composed of acutely trained persons dedicated to the aims of helping peace and justice return to the world. The fellowship blends with many other worlds, many kinds of personalities and persons, for what concerns one of God's creatures concerns us all. An infinitude of souls are collaborating in this endeavor from many worlds and many kinds of worlds."

Thought Reconstructs

"The thought reconstructs are only temporarily real, but able to give advice, instruction and information. Such a personality draws its intermittent life from cosmic consciousness. It is perceived by those who are able in their superconscious, but it is not always perceived by their consciousness. Perhaps that is more of a confusion than an explanation, but it is the best we can do at this moment. When you learn more about the superconscious, the meaning will come unraveled."

Legendary Ones

"The legendary ones who are called up by the method of thought reconstruct also have "life" for a temporary period. The man who saw the warty fellow with the pointed ears and green cap at the foot of his garden saw a "real" existence, but real only for the period of time he was needed, that is, only for as long as he was held in the mind of the person who called him up. Nature spirits, Pan, centaurs, all of these legendary creatures can be called "forth" by the one adept at such abilities.

"At this time the only others we can explain who appear on our list are the energy existences, but this explanation will help answer many, many questions that you have in your minds."

Energy Existences

"We have said that we, ourselves, the UFO people, are as human and corporeal as yourselves, but we can also have being in other alternate states, as energy existences in our psychic essence and as semi-corporeal personalities. When we are in our psychic essence state, correspondent to your out-of-body experience, we can image ourselves into a world that is co-existent and co extensive to your own, existing in the same space, but in a different time dimension. At such a time we merely use the realities of this coexistent world as much as it is convenient for us to do so.

"However, this world and its very real inhabitants exist very well without our intervention, and we shall describe and delineate this world and its personalities as they exist in themselves.

"In this world there are beings of several degrees of complexity, from almost one-dimensional creatures to highly complex souls who have chosen never to be born into a physical world."

Messengers

"We shall take up first those one-dimensional creatures that are a clan of organizers and obtainers. These have the attribute of psychic existence and that is all. They serve as messengers and thing bringers to those who have more complex being or to those who have come into this world on an errand or for a purpose temporarily.

"They are not as observable as a wisp of smoke or fog, not even that much. They would be more as a wave of energy or a very slow whirlwind of energy. Their sole purpose is to serve other, more complex and purposeful beings."

Psychic Connectives

"The next, little more complex personalities in this co-existent world are the personalities who take charge of psychic experience when sought by an Earth individual. Did you think you did it all by yourself? No, these are the connecting link between the searching individual and the manifestation he is trying to bring about.

"These personalities, although individual and quite conscious and "knowing," are not indicated by names, for there is no need to tell one from other. All are the same in every respect, just as all molecules of water are the same. Each one can perform exactly the same function as the next. If they are pursuing a task one time, they do not in the least need to return to it later. Any one of their number will simply fit himself into the job at hand and do it equally well. Their memory is all one, a kind of memory bank on which all draw whatever information is needed to continue.

"Because we have had centuries of experience working with them, we are able to use them easily, and I think, quite wisely. We simply direct their efforts so they fit our needs."

Pseudo-demons and Inspirators

"The third level of personalities in this psychic world are those who do have names, are self-directed and who can be very helpful or very mischievous depending on their whim. They can manifest themselves corporeally if they desire to do so, and sometimes do, taking on any shape or appearance they desire. It is not a permanent appearance, though it may persist for some time until they tire of it and go on to something else. All of this is very startling, confusing and, of course, frightening to any human witness.

"The mischievous ones are what we might call pseudo-demons and at times they can be most disruptive and even harmful to human beings.

"However there are helpful ones from this area also, and their aid can be very beneficial and useful indeed.

"We depend a very great deal on this third level of psychic existences and mingle and work with them when we are in our psychic essence manifestation. Their character and abilities then are very much like our own when we are in that state. We converse by pictorial telepathy and move about in their world quite as freely as they do themselves.

"At such times we do not have the use of our physical senses to the same extent we do in the physical world. We do not detect odor or color. The great advantage we find in this world is that it exists in a different time dimension than your own. Time is simply non-existent in your idea of mechanistic time. That is, it can be so stretched or so shrunk that it no longer has any meaning.

"These personalities are not spirits but are as souls who have never been born, vastly evolved souls, very sophisticated and very complex. They are wise with a wisdom of incredible eons of experience. Their efforts in your behalf are many; they are supportive of many of your endeavors and serve to guide and protect. You reach them by means of supplication to whatever gods, great or little, that you pray to. This is their purpose, to aid you in all your activities. You are fortunate to be able to attract the most evolved ones relative to your own evolutionary status.

"They live by stringent laws and may not impose their own ideas or purposes on anyone in your world. In their endeavors to aid the people of your world we have called them the inspirators.

"Most people are helped in this interior fashion as long as they keep their minds open to reception. Some are very delicately attuned to reception; some resist with all their might."

Instructors

"Of the same purpose as the inspirators are the instructors. Everyone has them to one degree or another. You can equate the reception of the work of the inspirators and the instructors with your mental in-take, and while the capacity for this is in your inheritance, it is not altogether dependent on your heredity. From the instant you are born you start to choose, accept or reject the various stimuli that come to you. By this use of your own free will, you contribute to your evolution as a soul. You are endowed with a soul at birth; it is not inherited through your physical ancestors.

"The variance between the inspirators and the instructors is that the latter are every bit as human and corporeal as yourself!

"The instructors inhabit many worlds and many places. In some worlds their work is secret and unknown, as it is for the most part on Earth. In other worlds they work openly and freely among those who have learned and who accept their presence and aid.

"The instructors hold and condense the knowledge of the Universe. All will be passed on to Earth people when you are able and willing to accept it.

"The instructors carefully guide and guard through the aid of the inspirators who make the direct contacts.

"We have used their world and their aid to contact and develop many persons in your world. All have been chosen years ago and are waiting, without knowing, for our call to come forth Someday all will be told."

Questions

1.   Do you feel that you have reached an apex or climax in your greater task?

2.   What event or incident made you realize you had reached a kind of summit?

3.   Did you feel this was in any way a more than natural event? Describe.

4.   Have the aggravating tests type of event diminished after this?

5.   Do you now feel a sense of collaborating with the SBs? Describe.

6.   Have you been given names of your communicators? Describe their general personality as much as you have been able to discern such.

7.   Describe any experiences with what might have been out-of-body presences.

8.   Have you experienced anyone in a semi-corporeal state as far as you can tell?

9.   Relate any other experiences you feel that you have had with psychic existences or beings in a psychic state.

Our initiand here is looking to the left at some complicated communication devices and in his hand holds his new power to control strange and wonderful forces which we might guess to signify psychic forces.

CHAPTER TEN

Special Abilities

When we come to the special abilities of the contactee, we find that they often take the form of psychic abilities. If we go to past and current literature on the subject, we discover the outstanding exhibit of all time is probably Uri Geller.

Uri's stage presentations are just that, staged presentations, coupled, I believe, with a sly sense of humor. But Uri has undergone extensive scientific examinations by many at Stanford Research Institute and elsewhere, and his amazing abilities seem to hold up under the most severe inspection.

Spoon bending and watch stopping are by no means all there is to his abilities. I do often wonder, however, how people from his audience who have had their car keys bent manage to drive home, or how those with bent door keys get into their apartments.

Uri is accredited with such feats as stopping escalators in stores and cable cars on mountains and repairing electronic devices or watches that had been stopped for years, all with mind concentration. He has bent heavy steel rods as well as spoons, and he has made objects disappear and reappear, levitate and so much more. He has said the source of his power comes from outside himself, that he is a channel and the ability that comes through him is directed from other intelligence. And he tells of names and places.

Uri has been fortunate to have had the guidance and counsel of Dr. Andrija Puharich, who has certainly saved him many a misstep, mishap and surely the usual mistakes of the novice. His development has thus been quicker and his abilities more easily displayed than an untutored contactee.

I am sure that the public has not been informed of the best of his powers, but we have seen enough to make us aware that psychic ability has great potential and that we are able to manipulate the physical through the powers of the mind. It may take the earthling generations to regain his intended psychic abilities in full measure, although the SBs are waiting to help us regain some of our lost inheritance.

Many contactees, not so well known nor so flamboyant as Uri Geller, find themselves able to use paranormal abilities after a sustained course of UFO encounters.

Many go into psychic healing work, many become mediums of one kind or another, many continue with automatic writing or drawing or telepathic writing, while others become involved in psychic research itself. Some research into such events as haunted houses and ghostly appearances or undertake to cleanse homes of poltergeists. Some are fascinated with the idea of psychic archeology. Some find that they have become subjects of such events as levitation, out-of-body experiences and far viewing. Others begin to "dream true" of things that later happen. Many develop an uncanny ability to know who is on the phone or at the door before they answer the ring. Some "just know" when they will receive an important letter or feel that they should telephone some friend or relative, only to find this was for a momentous reason.

These abilities have been developing over the period of time when the contacts have been taking place, and they come to full recognition about the time of the final act of initiation.

The total meaning of a UFO event is complex and complicated. There is much more than a single purpose going on. We can compare this to the difference between a hollow plastic ball and a ball of cord that someone has been saving for years. No UFO event or SB contact is as singular as the plastic ball with smooth sides and nothing but air inside. It is like the ball of wound twine, many colors and sizes tied together and all lying in a crisscross, back and forth, in and out, forming a geometric design of meaning and purpose.

Each experience is enormously complex, representing many levels of meaning, various conditions of reality and accomplishing a whole multitude of ends, all of this lying under the surface of the event itself, just as the multi-colored strings lie at various levels below the surface of the wrapped ball of twine.

Thus there is no single interpretation of any one event. Just as there are differences between the beneficial and the mischievous psychic existences, so there are differences in the uses of psychic abilities.

By the time these abilities are ready for "public" use, the SBs know full well how they are going to be used. The contactee after all, as Uri said, is only a channel, and if he does not perform according to the rules, he will have his water cut off. He will find the psychic energies no longer flow through him, and the SBs no longer use him as a channel. Perhaps as they leave him to his own devices, the mischievous ones take over to his detriment and to his despair. Uri has had some troubles of his own, perhaps along this line.

There is an unspoken question that my contact, Hweig, wants me to clarify before I forget again. Where and how do the SBs get the symbols they use to put across ideas to us, like the contactees who were given the symbols of men in suits of armor? From the contactee's subconscious. Where else would they find the residue of his cultural past? The subconscious of each of us contains not only the past of our current life, but the residue of all of our former incarnations from our year 0000000000001 (the number is different for each of us).

They try to use symbols from our current life, as these are the ones that can be recalled to consciousness most easily, just as we do for the most part in our dreams. The subconscious records mainly by pictorial symbols, but not altogether, and there are limitations here as well.

The SBs, or their psychic helpers, dig into our subconscious with the definite idea that they eventually want us to come up with. The subconscious responds with the closest symbol it can find in its vast inventory. Did you think the subconscious meant unconscious? Think again; it is simply a different condition of consciousness, one we are seldom aware of except in dreams, visions, *etc.* We simply could not hold everything that happens to us constantly in conscious awareness. Much more is to be distilled and stored.

Then the SBs use the symbol that we ourselves have projected from our subconscious in such a manner that it becomes perceived once again by our everyday kind of consciousness. This consciousness then must interpret the symbol by recalling the historical origin of the symbol and thus convert it back into the idea.

Why the long way around? Why not a short cut of exhortation or even threatening? For several reasons I can think of, and no doubt a number I know nothing about. Principally, because they are not permitted to put ideas directly into our minds—they have to use subterfuges and camouflage.

To me this sounds awfully close to quibbling, but if their conscience and their superiors permit them to get away with such circumlocutions, I shall not argue. I am sure there are reasons for this roundabout method.

We pay closer attention to what has been called into our own minds and more easily accept it as truth, since it seemed to come out of ourselves, and we keep on thinking about it longer, once it has been presented to us in this staged manner. And, since our subconscious has already gone through the exercise of digging up the symbol, our consciousness should not be so hard put to make the subconscious cough up the idea behind the symbol. It has already been oiled for action.

In short, there are more reasons than I could ever think of for this manner of presentation of an idea. I acquiesce that those SBs know what they are doing, and that is their worry. I have enough of my own.

The SBs gave me the following interpretation of their beginning interactions with me:

"You were first picked up on our research instruments, as all of our contacts are, then analyzed and followed with our recording devices and finally impelled, with the aid of the energy existences, to use the pendulum. Many other people are being surveyed and coaxed by one means or another to make or to find contact with us.

"A great number of our scientists now work with persons here on earth trying to bring them to a condition of usefulness for the purpose of making direct contact and physical landings. Your people are not emotionally prepared for us, not nearly as much as we had hoped.

"We have come to the conclusion that the only way we can make direct contact without being shot down is by revealing truths about ourselves. By doing it in such manner as this, we are not putting our lives in jeopardy.

"There is so much we cannot reveal until we are sure of our reception among your people. We are not allowed to initiate, instigate or create thoughts, ideas or beliefs in your mind. But once these come into your thoughts through books, TV, movies or by your own analysis, we are able to verify, strengthen and to some extent expand the idea or thought.

This is why you complained that what we told you always seemed to be only an echo of something you have known elsewhere. Under telepathy we cannot initiate new ideas. If we could talk to you directly, we could tell you anything.

"We want at all times to emphasize the difference between psychic and spiritual. We never dreamed there could be so much confusion between the two. We, the UFO people, deal in psychic matters. There are others who bring you information on spiritual matters. This does not concern us, except to warn you not to allow a cult or religion to arise based on the things we tell you. No cults! No religions!

"We choose those we want to reach by a very scientific analysis. You are watched and analyzed for a very long time but not interfered with, for that would render the analysis useless.

"When we have selected one we wish to reach we send out energy impulses that are thought forms. These are pictorial representations, but since your psychic centers are not open, you receive these as urges or compulsions.

"Our initial attempt at reaching you, before you used the pendulum, was to send a shower of energy waves, directed specifically at you. You felt it as an urge to try to contact whatever was out there. Whenever we note even a spark of interest such as this, we send out more and more and more impulses until you feel compelled to investigate.

"Since we made contact with you through the pendulum, let us follow how that works. As soon as you took up the pendulum, suggested to you by a fellow worker, we tried to implant suggestions for its better use. Soon you drew an alphabet around a circle so we could use actual words in response to your questions. I am afraid in our eagerness to "develop" you we overstepped bounds and gave you some bad times.

"After we impelled you to use the pendulum, we had to move it, of course. This is done by direct impulses, or waves of energies, directed at the pendulum itself. It has nothing to do with subconscious or involuntary muscular action. Any jerking of the muscles is due to the muscular tension, letting go, relaxing, in one jump. Fatigue, excitement, or other emotions cause a too tight pinch on the cord, which does not allow it to swing freely.

"The person watching the pendulum becomes the victim of hypnosis, which opens the mind for telepathy.

"At first you asked your questions aloud, and the vibrations of the voice were picked up by a kind of psychic antenna. It is not actually that, but we shall so label it for the present.

"The vibrations of your voice are an energy transmission to which we are tuned with our psychic receivers, which you have as well but don't know how to use yet. You will be taught.

"At first, the vibrations of voice are necessary. Later, after we have learned your mode of speech and connotations, which are different for each you will be able to transmit thought vibrations without the actual voice. You will not realize what or how you are doing this, until we have time to teach you more about it. Either kind of vibration is picked up by us and translated into symbols regardless of your language or any impediment of speech for actually it is the energy pattern of thought that comes through. At first these patterns are registered by a chart or graph. (We have a permanent record of everything you think!) Once we have learned your particular thought patterns and their meanings, we can receive them directly into our minds even as you are transmitting them directly from your mind. A perfect telepathy has been established. All of this is much simpler than our labored explanation sounds!

"Automatic writing may start before you are able to receive our communication in return. Once telepathy has been established, the automatic writing can turn to telepathic writing, which seems to be nothing more nor less than dictation from us. Whatever the exact process proves to be for each of you, we are soon conversing in your own vernacular or idiom, either by pen or voice, or both.

"By that time we have been able to measure very accurately your potential use to us and to your fellow man. We have a pretty good understanding of your potentials as psychic researchers and a profound judgment of your character.

"Our requirements are strict, only a small portion of neophytes become initiates, and very few become adepts. This is not entirely through their own limitations, but through ours as teachers. We strive to avoid former mistakes and vow to do better in the future."

Questions

1.   Do you believe that you have developed psychic abilities as a result of your cooperation or collaboration with the SBs? Describe and fit your development of psychic abilities into the time frame of your overall experiences.

2.   Do you feel that you have developed any other abilities, or that you have been inspired to study, research and train in other fields due to UFO contacts?

3.   Can you reveal any special information or instructions you have received relative to developing paranormal abilities?

4.   What was your introduction to the field of psychic experiences relative to UFOs?

5.   Do you feel that you have derived any personal benefit from your psychic experience?

6.   Do you have plans for the future in the psychic fields?

The climax of the initiation is elevation to a higher order, a greater level of responsibility. The spiral of ascent is on this personage's chest, but covered over by levels of experience and knowledge that he has passed through. He has arrived. The flames of enlightenment, or spirituality, come from his shoulders like wings.

CHAPTER ELEVEN

Elevation

The final act of the initiatory process is to give the initiand, who is now the initiate, elevation into an area of greater freedom, but at the same time, greater responsibility. You may not hear a word or find any unusual event at this point, but you will know it by a sudden euphoria and a feeling of having been "let out of a box." Feelings of constraint, which you had grown so used to you hardly noticed them, will lift.

Depending upon your particular type of experience, you can feel this euphoria, to the point of ecstasy, as Betty Andreasson went into a marvelous release of ecstasy at the revelations of the radiance.

The young woman who went to the Maya country, alone, said that when she came to a certain pyramid, she "flew" to the top and felt as though she could fly off into space, although as a rule she had some difficulty trudging up the exceedingly steep and broken steps of the pyramids. It was her moment of euphoria, I am sure, although she states that she does not feel she has "finished" an initiation, perhaps only one "degree."

For myself, this release of restraint has been a recent occurrence when I felt myself suddenly freed. Although I still hope to collaborate with the good forces that guide me, I am not so coerced into specific activities, but am permitted greater freedom to choose for myself. In other words, I can say "No" without a knock-down drag-out fight about it.

This might mean I am so indoctrinated with their propaganda that I choose to do what they would want anyway. No, I don't think that is so. They did not suggest I write this book, for instance, and have been pressuring me all the way through to hurry and get done with it, for they had something else in mind for me to do.

If they have mental contact, much can be explained to you at this point, although they prefer you to figure some things out for yourself. You may even have a little ritual of elevation. Each experiences according to his own role in the total event, and by the sort of thing that would speak to him most eloquently.

The whole process of initiation has been reduced to such a personal thing that it is difficult to give more than a bare outline to follow or explain. Each contactee can fill in the particulars of his own experience. We hope that by answering the questions, you have been able to follow some of the tangible evidence of a real meaning in the events that have come to you, or even been forced upon you, on occasion.

Along with your time of elevation should come a feeling of rightness in what you are doing. By this time you should be, must be, convinced that you are working for a good and noble purpose at your selected task. There will be some back sliding of doubt as you read or hear arguments against this, but you will worry it through and come out once again confident of the validity of what you have chosen and been guided to do.

You will also know that in a moment of serious indecision or actual danger you will be guided and protected. You may not hear a word, but you will "just know" the right course to follow. You have not been abandoned; you have been set free.

You will even be able to input observations and ideas into the total event. You will be listened to, though not necessarily hailed as a genius. You have become a valuable collaborator, not just a drag, squawking and protesting.

Staunch skepticism has long delayed my own progress to this point. There are still so many unanswered questions. Maybe now I can discover more meaning, more reasons.

From this point you will advance by "degrees" in study, research, knowledge, understanding and, I hope, travel. As always it will require great application and honorable resolve.

By this time you are repeating your question, "What have I been initiated into?" The answer to this question is vital to your mental equilibrium and to your sustained application to your task.

We have mentioned, "a fellowship of acutely trained persons dedicated to the aims of helping peace and justice return to this world." And in Chapter 1 of Part II, we have further explained the specific ways in which they intend to help us rejuvenate the earth and aid in the evolution of Man.

Well now! Where does this organization exist? Is it piece meal with participants like yourself scattered across the world, hardly recognizing themselves, let alone each other? Or is there some mark of identification, some place or places of meeting or some surface communication other than the mental ones?

Yes indeedy, all of these.

And you will find these, one by one, as you progress through your succeeding efforts. Different sources will become available to you, specially chosen for your unique needs. A vast network of collaborators exists throughout the world. One by one those you are to work with will come to your attention. You will be given clues, and sometime later even secrets that you will not divulge.

In the past, contactees were deliberately kept apart. Each was told to guard the material they had been given, to await the "signal" to release it. Each was made a little suspicious of other known contactees. The area of material given to each was so unique that it did not seem to coordinate with any other. Each contactee, when nearly ready "to come out," was made to appear strange, disordered or ridiculous, thus making his validity suspect. Each contactee was given only a portion of the puzzle, the key to unlocking its full meaning was deliberately withheld. Each was given both sides of a problem, the yea and nay, without being shown how to polarize the two. This kept him confused and off balance, never able to reach certainty. Contactees were often "teased" just enough to keep them skeptical of the purposes of their informant. Some were warned against forming clubs or cults or any group that would involve making comparisons and exchanging their given material. Thus, no complete fitting of patterns could take place. Contactees were made to forget the cohesive parts of their material. These were left buried in the subconscious, barring slippages in dreams or under hypnosis, until the day of revelation would be at hand. Contactees received overt warnings, threats, adjurations to remain silent and to reveal their experiences in no public manner, thereby cutting off the possibility of material being shared and compared too soon.

But quietly, underneath all this camouflage, subterfuge, and general concealment, a quiet, steady, sustained coherent network was forming, partly through the machinations of the SBs and their colleagues and partly through the understanding, analysis, and retention of ideas by the contactees themselves. More and more rapidly, always steadily, the network was taking form, day by day, minute by minute, all over the world, unseen, unknown, unguessed, until in these last few years there begins to surface here and there, always quietly, always subdued, but always steadily, evidence that such a network did exist and was being deliberately planned by the SBs themselves, with the unconscious collaboration of the contactees.

Here and there the network of threads is showing through, the elaborate skeins of significance that tie one contactee to another. The vital juncture points, the knots, are of world significance, vital to the future well-being of all the Earth's inhabitants and perhaps to those mysterious inhabitants of unseen worlds as well!

Formed from the cultural environment in which they came to be, each thread was an interpretation of the meaning of life and the universe relative to that contactee's time and place. In the beginning the threads were relative to Man and his relationship to Nature. The threads now being formed are relative to Man as world being, and will stretch into the future of Man as cosmic being.

The juncture points, or "knots," of the network are the places or ideas where various contactees can compare and bring together their individual experiences and information. Each contactee will find that he has juncture points with many other contactees, but there is a definite distribution pattern, a definite *design* to the network. It is not a helter- skelter disarray of tangled threads.

The cohesive factor or force that ties it all together is a new understanding of Man's place in the cosmic scheme of things. It is being revealed in the emergence of knowledge of the *psychic* realities that have been thought of previously as magic, occult, supernatural or superstition. The new revelation of man's place in the physical universe of things is through quantum physics and the new mathematics. A new science/religion or religion/science will become more obvious in the near future; it is slowly coming into observation even now.

To the contactee as a private man, the network could mean a way of fulfilling his basic needs: finding his place in his immediate environment, or changing his environment; becoming absorbed in his own value and meaning; looking for productive relationships with other contactees; re-adjusting his life direction or intent; strengthening his will or motivation; re-assigning his hours to more productive ends; gaining in self-confidence and courage, re-affirming faith in some greater power or plan or purpose.

How many contactees in the United States alone are even now restructuring their lives because of a UFO contact? I am sure we would all be surprised to learn that number!

The value of the network to the world Man could mean gaining understanding and knowledge through comparisons with other's experiences; consolidating work with others, through apportionment of studies, saving time and energy for all; learning many facets and values of experience in addition to one's own; and extension of knowledge through parallels, analogies and patterns.

The value of the network to cosmic Man: the contactee views the person he is to become, the culmination of the whole process. He sees his personal place in the universe, the cosmic scheme, his relationship to beings from another planet, other time worlds, other energy worlds and parallel (space) worlds; he sees his significance to infinite/eternal verities and realities, in contrast to their significance to him.

As the contactee/researcher comes to analyze and understand the contactee experience and to compare one with another contactee, he will begin to see a definite pattern of distribution in types of experience. This is not a geographical distribution, but one made patent by the character attributes of the contactees. As long as the researchers look for repetitive patterns of experience, they are going in the wrong direction. They must find their patterns for research in the basic character of the contactee and in their patterns of belief.

More than this I cannot reveal at this time, mostly because I do not know more. I know the future will be exciting and bring worthwhile adventures, as long as I do my best and conform to the same standard that I have set for myself up to this point. It has succeeded so far, and with extension and refinement the same standard will carry me into the future. Step by step is the only way to proceed.

I have now brought you up to the point of my own understanding of the initiatory process, and so I must close this section of the book, except for some final questions, and for a brief summing up and conclusion.

Thank you for bearing with me. May it be to your benefit.

Questions

1.   At what point do you feel you now stand in the process of initiation?

2.   Do you feel that your life has been improved by your participation? In what way?

3.   If you had a choice, would you want to continue?

4.   Do you feel totally committed to the task you have undertaken?

5.   Do you feel a little "elevated," more sure of who you are and where you are going?

6.   Do you feel more powerful to help others?

7.   Have you had a conversion of attitudes toward certain persons, organizations or philosophies?

8.   Do you feel you have been "let out of the box" and are now proceeding more freely by your own desires, needs, understanding and choices? Describe.

Comment on any aspect of your own initiatory process as you wish. Try to date or indicate the time element of experiences. This is the end of direct questions. Add any comments you like.

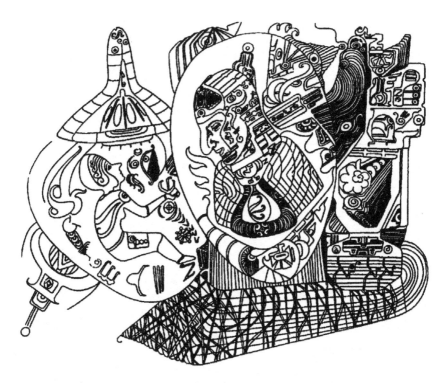

So *many things are summed up here—human relationships, relations to growing things, flowers, plants. Something above the girl's hand looks like a lyre, indicative of culture. There are things of art and science. Flames of spirituality are also shown.*

So many things!

CHAPTER TWELVE

Summary

To summarize our exposition of the initiatory process we must stick to the general outline of the process itself. Individual experiences of initiation are entirely too individual to help us here.

The fact that certain initiatory events in the contactee's life have been wiped out of consciousness for a period of time makes a chronological recall of the individual process difficult. Perhaps the various ideas we have introduced throughout will help bring many of those events into consciousness once again.

The first overt act of initiation, the separation of the initiand, can be recognized rather easily. It brings considerable distress and uneasiness into his/her mind. He finds himself alone and fighting off the SBs on one hand and his relatives and neighbors with the other. He stands helpless as a kind of sounding board between the two, seemingly attacked from both sides and powerless to ward off the blows and hurts. This is the first and most necessary step to pry the contactee loose from his past, his mistaken misconceptions, misadventures and misunderstandings. Since we do not live forever, the separation and subsequent retraining must be done in some haste, sometimes brusquely, almost brutally. There is little time to waste on coaxing or sweet talking. On with the job!

Introduction into a circular enclosure is mostly a ritual act, though of course there is a practical purpose in getting him somewhere desired. It is symbolic and traditional, a marking out of intention, a kind of clue to the contactee, if such has been brought to his attention. If not, it will be, and he will understand its meaning and purpose. He enters into the womb of change as a man of nature for a period of gestation that will be followed by his rebirth as a man of social conscience, as well as social consciousness, the cultural man or woman. He will become an active participant in the new order of the coming age.

The symbols that the contactee sees can be interpreted by him with a little deep thinking, for these symbols have been drawn forth from the repository of his subconscious by methods those SBs are practiced at using. They have carefully chosen not to inform of these at present, but they promise to elucidate and even teach us as we become ready and able to learn.

It is because these symbols are drawn from the subconscious of each contactee that it would seem to an observer that he was "making it all up." Believe me, we would not put ourselves through the hell and hassle of contacteeship just to be tough on ourselves! We would never choose the events and experiences we go through for our own amusement.

Perhaps our guides, instructors or mentors have chosen each of us for the challenge we provide. Are we so noncompliant, so obtuse, so far off the track that to retrain us would be a feather in their professorial cap? We must have some attraction, offer some challenge, or contain some desirable potential to make them choose us and to stay with us for the duration.

How many hours, days, weeks, months, and years does the full course require? Yet, these mentors are patiently there, good natured for the most part, unless we try too meanly to kick over the traces. They plod along day after day at our side, holding the carrots in front of the donkey's nose. Surely they must tire of the task also, and wish it would soon end, so they could retire and go about their business elsewhere. Are we such a joy and a prize that they would want to live with us and our cantankerousness forever?

I know I owe my Hweig many thanks and great appreciation for his unequaled patience. He only yelled "Shut up!" at me once when I was teasing him by talking, talking, talking when he was trying to say something that he thought was important.

Disciplines, ordeals and vows are tedious, frustrating and sometimes terrifying. They were meant to be. What good is a discipline if it is not tedious and frustrating? It must be overcome by patience, endurance and a calm attitude. It is no discipline if it lacks application and endeavor, and as such would be of no value.

If an ordeal holds not one bit of fright, it is simply hard work and no ordeal. Vows test one's integrity, trustworthiness and sense of responsibility. The better we come through all this, the greater advancements are possible and more inspiring the tasks we are given.

Studying the cultural and spiritual traditions of the world makes a man more of a man, and a woman more of a woman. Now he/she contains a breadth and depth of vision unrealized previously. The former cramped vision held of mankind has become expansive and comprehensive. Now the contactee has greater possibilities of analysis and choice. By so much have we enlarged ourselves and our potentials.

The particular task we have undertaken, creative, scientific or technological, has become a way of life to us and will surely be an asset in our future. Perhaps it is an entirely new sense of direction, or perhaps it is a long-abandoned activity that we have now taken up anew and will develop to a valuable usefulness. We will never regret it, but we will come to be grateful as well as gratified.

Our previous life will come to be seen as a dark forest through which we stumbled haphazardly. Now we emerge into the sunlight and find well laid-out trails leading securely into our future.

A sense of quietude and peace comes upon us. We can begin to relax a little, look around us once again and enjoy twice more what we find.

There are always questions. One must ever be wary and never become lulled into carelessness and foolishness.

Last warning: don't go to sleep on the trail or a dinosaur may step on you! Instead of belonging to the future, you will be overtaken by the past.

Powers and abilities beyond the chosen task, or as an outgrowth thereof, is the reward of the initiate. To be able to do something we never could before, to be recognized where before there was only indifference or to be able to give something freely that had been hoarded before, such as love for our fellows—these are the rewards.

Elsewhere I have remarked that "elevation" to a contactee seems to be simply more work. Perhaps that is not entirely fair! I have found that it means being let loose, to be more of myself again, not so much held to the requirements of others. It is escape from bondage, not perfectly, but enough to make one feel a bit giddy .

For every yea there is a nay. If there were no night there could be no day. If we knew not sorrow, could we understand joy? That's the secret, you see, the balancing, finding the equilibrium. That is what it is all about.

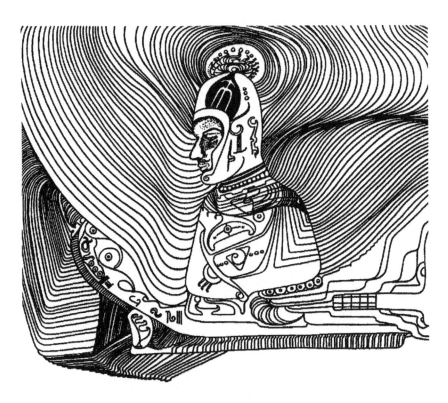

Here the initiate wears the flaming crown of enlightenment. He is surrounded by the energies of spiritual thought and being.

The way through the path of initiation has clarified the route to a more spiritual sense of being.

CHAPTER THIRTEEN

Conclusion

Contactees have been much maligned in the past and totally unable to protect themselves. Of course they could not explain what was happening to them; it was too bizarre and too frightening, and it came on much too rapidly and repetitiously. Before the poor fellow could analyze what had just happened, something new was banging him on the head.

This was done purposely to keep him from adding two and two together before it was time for him, and others, to know the why's and wherefores.

Once the contactee has been set free and is able to regain composure and recapitulate events, he may begin to understand the design of the purpose of the events and may thereby come to some meaning. The major meanings he will discover are the changes, advancements and development of character and his own aims and purposes.

He has spread. He has become larger than life. He is now able to make himself seen and known as something other than a nut. In most instances he has developed into something of a psychic. Not the newspaper or tabloid kind of psychic exhibitionist, but a quiet, behind-the-scenes researcher into psychic realities. If he can find a scientist, well trained and interested in helping guide his developing resources, he is indeed fortunate. His progress will be eased and shortened, and it will all be given more credence than if he were traveling alone. But he will go it alone if necessary.

His understanding now will expand to a worldwide basis, and he will experience a long period of discovery.

Dawn Man was perhaps the greatest man-psychic bom on earth, for he encapsulated in purest unadulterated form his inheritance from the "sons of gods" who had mated with the "daughters of men." This is more than a figure of speech and far more than a Biblical myth. Such stories go far, far back in prehistory, long before the Semitic language was even invented. But the Semitics drew upon facts of so long before their own time that the time element became confused as the stories had been told, and told and re-told.

Throughout the course of man's history, the purity of psychic ability was so adulterated, turned to evil purposes— the so called occult—that at length it was all but lost. To recapture some of these abilities is not impossible for the centers in the brain, and the encoding in the genes is still there in all perfection! It is only a matter of retraining in a wholesome and healthful manner.

Hallucinogens and tantric sex may work in limited degree to develop a psychic so attuned, but these are not the way to real control; they are a way of enforcement rather than collaboration. To control the powers one must collaborate, not demand or try to wrench them forcibly from the psychic realities that contain them.

If a contactee's heart and mind are set upon making a fair exchange, the opportunity will be given him. This does not mean selling one's soul to the devil!

If a contactee has a firm conviction of the reality and justice of God and has made for himself the sternest moral discipline he can conceive, he need have no fear of undertaking a collaborative development of his psychic abilities. Even the pseudo-demons we spoke of will come to respect his integrity and leave him alone. They only torment those who leave the door open.

If you are overwhelmed by those beasties at any time, grab a Bible and read the twenty-third psalm over and over and over, fervently cleaving to every word. (Or whatever book or verse is comparable in your own belief.) The pseudos will respectfully withdraw; they are not mindless and not actually cruel. They are only bored and cannot find anything better to do.

Exorcism and exhortation only infuriates them, and they can become rather violent. Distract their attention. Give them the idea of something more interesting to do, and they will skip happily off to a new activity.

Keep the door closed by concentrating your mind, not on them and their shenanigans, but on good and constructive thoughts.

No one can deny the efficacy of prayer and a joyful worship. Sing! Do not ask for something in fear, but give an offering of thanksgiving or as a commitment to service.

Truly it is difficult to know when one is having an induced illusion or, when driven by adverse circumstances, a real mental aberration.

It is possible at one time that my personal experience with hallucination was more than an induced event. I had been working with the pendulum, and I got into a streak where I could not put it down, night or day. For five days and nights I scarcely ate or slept, thus putting myself into perfect condition for a hallucination. Also, I had put myself into a constant state of hypnosis by watching the pendulum with such severe concentration. And, as we have related, hypnosis is the door to all psychic phenomena. There came whispers in my ear telling me all sorts of unnerving things. I was being "watched" from various places by various means, and finally that I was about to be blown up by enemies. At that I did the only sensible thing I could think of in my rattled state—I went to the police for protection. It was a total disaster. If I had eaten and slept properly, it never would have happened. Perhaps the compulsion that drove me to the sleepless days and nights was deliberately planned to bring about the hallucination. I do not know how much was planned, and how much was my own stupidity.

If it was deliberately planned, I am sure it was for a purpose. I have not yet learned to appreciate that! It blew my life apart at the seams. Still, after I was feeling myself once more, the richest, most productive part of my life began. From my viewpoint, everything got better.

If your own experience has precipitated a breakdown, or you feel on the borderline, calm down. Erase the fear, and half the problem will vanish.

The more you try to convince people that you are not crazy, the more they will convince themselves that you are. Keep calm. Don't argue. As your life progresses and you have the witness of many good works to your credit, their evaluation will change. Anyone who has not been through a similar experience cannot possibly understand. Don't expect them to, and you cannot be disappointed. We needed to add these warnings of some of the pitfalls you may run afoul of during your course of contacteeship. Being forewarned, you can meet them with better common sense than I managed to show. I was completely in the dark as to how such manifestations came about and how to deal with them. I hope the recital of my own shortcomings and mishaps will steer you away from similar problems, or at least give you a hint of what to do should something arise.

In Part II of this book we have dealt mainly with the process of initiation as the contactee will discover it in his own experience. But, as stated, initiation is only a part of the total experience.

Reading this book, you have an opportunity to respond to my suggestions and thus help to clarify a portion of your own UFO experience. To get your story all laid out in one place can only help substantiate those wisps and vapors that would not pin down to any sensible interpretation

If we still have queasy feelings in our stomachs that the final purpose of the SBs may not be what we would choose, we still have not committed ourselves to an irreversible course of action. We have gained, and gained well for ourselves, but we are still able to weigh, judge, evaluate and say "Whoa! So far and no farther!"

If we publish our findings in whatever manner seems advisable and possible, we have recorded a means of evaluation that others may consider, and from the total may come a method of study and eventually an understanding of what some of the final answers are. The phenomenon is there, willy nilly, whether we approve or not. We are caught in the events whether we like it or not. Buying the facts is not going to help us, or anyone, find reasons and purposes, or to devise means of controlling or counteracting the thrusting of such events upon us.

It behooves us, one and all, to reveal our experiences and information and to cooperate in deciding the total purposes and values of what we have experienced under the tutelage and interference of those SBs.

God keep us all—the contactees, the SBs, and the dedicated and unsung scientists and investigators who have spent so many years recording the ever bizarre stories that we tell, no matter how unbelievable or impossible they may sound.

P. S. Alice in Wonderland: "There's no use trying," she said, "One can't believe in impossible things."

"I daresay you haven't had much practice," said the (Red) Queen. "When I was your age I always did it for half an hour a day. Why, sometimes I believed in as many as six impossible things before breakfast!"

Part III
The Psychic World

Hweig Introduces

The Psychic World

The soul is not inherited through your physical ancestors. It is an endowment waiting for your physical appearance. You, Ida, have often commented that you felt a civil war inside yourself. Many have felt this. It is the battle of the physical instincts of the inherited physical attributes with the endowed soul.

Yes, you have a soul, and yes, it is immortal. But the soul itself is not divine. There you can prepare for many a battle. The divinity that can be glimpsed within a person is spirit, not soul; they are not synonymous. Soul is psychic, spirit is, well of course, spiritual. (That was an asinine sentence. I will interpolate and get myself into stupid utterances.) The spirit is from that which is divine, the ultimate God.

At the death of the body that which is divine returns to God, unsullied by human life. The soul, which is immortal, returns to its alternate life between lives, where it absorbs the lessons it has learned in the life just closed. No more on that at this time. We want to discuss another topic, the "world" of souls who have never been bom, a world that is co-existent and co-extensive to your own, existing in the same space, but in a different time dimension. It is *not* the world between lives; that is another world that we need not discuss at this time.

The world of unborn souls, psychic essences or energy existences is the one we want to reveal at this time, for it is a world that is in constant interaction with our world, and the personages of which have more influence on your own lives than you can ever imagine.

CHAPTER ONE

Psychic Essences Speak

Our area of being is coincident to your own. If we repeat, it is only so you can have the information all together. Our world, yes, our universe, is co-existent to yours. We live in the same area of space, but in a different time dimension. We are energy existences, not pure energy, but not very physical. Not at all physical as you know it. We are not angels. Perfection is not one of our attributes. We are not miracle workers. We have to work very hard at what we accomplish, perhaps much harder than you do. Our main interest in our "life" is to help persons on your level of understanding to reach a fuller and more refined understanding of reality. This is not synonymous with truth. Reality is a thing in itself. Not the reality of something, but reality itself. We do not wish to impose our ideas and purposes on anyone in your world. In fact, we cannot, or more exactly, may not. It is forbidden. Therefore, we have to wait until someone in your world actively seeks us, or seeks someone we think could be us, for sometimes they do not know precisely who or what they seek; they are only experimentally working to see if someone is there, as you, Ida, were experimenting with the pendulum. The person from your world has to actually ask for someone from some unknown other world to help them understand the many mysteries hidden from your knowledge. They may not say "someone"; they may ask for knowledge of a certain kind that we may give them. Then we are permitted to answer their seeking and try to find some way of making them understand what we have to offer.

Too many times the person seeking information is asking spirits of the dead to help them. We are not the spirits of the dead. We are energy existences; we are not persons like yourself; we have never been persons. We are not born, and we do not die. The closest we can explain it right now is to say we are like souls who have never been born. This is our own choice; we can come to this world or area of being if we freely choose. But we can never then change our mind and ask to be bom into the world. Or one who has been born and died can never come into our world. We can only tell you about ourselves, and you can experience many evidences of us.

Many women and men are too apt to stick to the deceased spirit idea and never can know us as we are able to present ourselves. You gave up the spirit idea long ago and accepted us as actual personages (not persons). Therefore, we have been able to present to you much understanding, and we experiment in developing more understanding. We have put much pressure on you in doing this, because we did not want you to have time to go back over your notes and put two and two together. At that time you would only get six. We wanted to wait until you had absorbed, rather unknowingly, many basic principles, and now we feel you have reached a point where we may work collaboratively with you to get it all together.

We do not have names here, as we do not have an actual language. It is difficult to get this across. We speak to each other and to you by telepathy, and that is not actually in words. You yourself translate into your language what we are putting across to you, and believe us, we do not have the slightest idea how you do it. You say it just comes to you in words, in English. Ah yes, and how do we get it back from you? In the same translation as we convey messages to each other. We do not actually hear words from you. We hear our own method of communication. Yes, you are right so far—the sound of words is in the vibration of the voice, our communication with each other is through energy vibrations—but this still does not clear up the mystery of how one is translated into the other.

We are experimenting with you, just as you are experimenting with us. Many times you have given us good ideas and hints that have enabled us to progress on this side very rapidly also.

Many times you have been angry with us, sometimes very angry, when we have misled or even outright told you falsehoods. Please believe me, these were very necessary red herrings across the trail so you did not guess too much too soon. It would be very dangerous for you to know too much before you knew how to control or use it.

We cannot say how much pleasure you have given many of us in allowing us to see places and things that have a great deal of interest to us for various reasons but which we could never see except through the eyes of someone like yourself. The little stop at the pet shop one day was a revelation to one here who has done a great deal of research in animals, birds, fishes and insects. You wonder why one who cannot see into your world would be interested in such things? Yes, you guessed it. He is then more fully able to help someone in your world who has problems that have to do with these things. Or places. Or people. Everything you show is grist to the mill for someone. To see them through your physical eyes as they appear in the physical world is something we never dreamed would be possible. Yes, others we have contacted and helped could do it for us, but they never developed to the point that they can do it so easily and consistently, and they usually do not take any interest in doing so, or in being cooperative and letting us know something in return for the knowledge we give them.

And that is the reason why you were so often given false information, misled and made to think and do certain futile and false things in the beginning. It was a test to see if you were going to help us in return; or if you only wanted to use us for your own benefit. Just like your own angry protestations, "I do not want to be just used!" You are so right to protest. And we protested in the only way we could that we did not like to be just "used." We refuse to give proper information to someone who was just after our knowledge without any thought as to our individuality, feelings or sensitivities. Yes, as you said today, we are perhaps more emotional than yourselves. We get our feelings hurt just as easily as you. But we have a job to do if we can. Therefore, we stick tightly with the person asking for help until he or she begins to see that it is a two-way street, that he can do something for us and that he is willing to do something for us also. In other words, the seeker must be willing to develop along the lines of good character and desire to help others also.

Never has anyone been so adept at understanding the problems that face us here. You seem to know our problems as well as we, and several times you have saved us from some kind of rather bad disaster with your suggestions. We do not know how you do this. You do not know how you do this. There are mysteries within mysteries here. We must continue to work on these hidden things together.

No, we neither eat nor sleep. We can work long stretches, but our energies do become depleted and we must take time to recuperate, but not so long as you need to sleep. As we have said, as energy existences, we neither eat nor sleep, but we must have recuperation from time to time.

Our idea of "time" is completely different from yours. It is not static or stationary in that it cannot be changed. We can manipulate our time any way we want. If we must wait for something to happen, we simply shrink time until a wait that might have been hours long becomes a few seconds. Or vice versa, if we have a tremendous amount of work we want to accomplish quickly, we can stretch time, so that a few minutes can stretch into several hours of work. But we can do this only for work or accomplishment. In other words, we can accomplish in a few minutes what actually takes hours and hours to do. That is as clearly as we can explain it right now.

We do not eat. What you might call nourishment to us is in the matter of restored energies and comes to us through means we have no way of describing. No, we don't hook ourselves up to a battery for recharging! Your method of utilizing forces in the world is still very primitive. Someday you will have much finer electrical forces to work with that will not necessitate much mechanical equipment. Electrical impulses and electromagnetic fields contain many secrets that you have not yet been able to uncover. You will know them all in time. We can help you start on the right road and will give you hints from time to time how to proceed. We are not permitted to do all the work for you, but we can be of tremendous help in pointing out roads to follow.

You asked how we can shrink or stretch time. Now is as good a time as any to explain just a little. We are able to do so because of particles that exist in space, which is your space as well as ours. These particles are of a sub-atomic nature, but your scientists have only begun to suspect their reality. They are the particles of pre-substance, which you wrote about in your outline,[6] not entirely energy, but barely aiming toward the physical, the first signs of matter or the first signs that matter will be possible. I fear this is becoming more of a confusion than an explanation. The particles exist in geometric time, even as you and I, but we are able to utilize it in ways in which you can scarcely conceive. This is really too difficult to get across.

---

6 *The Alien Book of Truth*, Ida Kannenberg, Wild Flower Press, 1992.

We are individuated existences, or you could call us entities, individuals, identities or personalities, but not persons, since that has connotations of physical being that we do not possess. But we do have minds or, in a sense, are beings of an energy substance of a nature almost parallel to mind itself. You do not have real comprehension of what "mind" is. You have demonstrated your knowledge of how it is used and where it exists, but not of the substance which gives it being. We cannot conversely say that we are all mind, for that is not at all true. But we are of a substance that is very close to the substance of which mind is constructed.

That is about all the information we can give on our substance of being at this time.

This does not mean we are super intelligences. We have to work for our knowledge as well as anyone else. We have had centuries in which to accumulate what we know, where you as persons have only a few years. We do have chronicles of our history and repositories of our knowledge, just as you have your libraries, books and now other media of preserving your knowledge for future generations. No individual in your area of being could learn it all from the beginning for himself, therefore you have to have these repositories of wisdom for each generation to draw from.

Of course the young always want to throw out what the old man has learned and do it all over again for himself, thus limiting himself and depriving himself of years of time when he might have been progressing instead of regressing. It is one of the frailties of human nature, yet it serves a purpose—it edits what has been learned. Every generation someone or other goes back through the wisdom of the past and weighs and measures what had been learned in one area or another and often is able to detect distortions or misunderstandings, which thereby can be corrected. So the rebel youth often make corrections that must be made if the path of future knowledge is not to be waylaid, blocked or sent off in wrong directions. There is a purpose for everything, even seeming disaster and injustice. If you could see everything from what you have called the opposite end of creation, that is, from the viewpoint of the Creator, the reason would be apparent and shown to be for the eventual good of the suffering individual. There is no way to show you this.

Our daily existence is not set off in hours as yours is. We do not have to rise from sleep and have breakfast as you do. Nor do we need to rest as much as you. We simply do a piece of work that interests us, and when it is finished we play until we feel the desire to work again. Our play is quite different from yours. We do not have sports, ball games, horse races or wrestling matches. It is indeed all mental sports or mental activities. We match our wits in what you would call games of intellect. And we do puzzles of a kind I do not know how to describe, since I have seen nothing in your world to correspond. But it is all mental. This is all we have to work or play with—our mental and emotional life. Yes, and well, I can't tell what most corresponds—I guess spiritual life, although we do not have religious beliefs or religions. We simply know what we are and what exists, and we accept these laws of being and try to collaborate with them. I suppose this takes the place of any religious life such as you have. You do not really know. We know. It is forbidden to discuss this topic with you to the extent of changing any ideas you previously possess. We can from time to time acknowledge when you have seen the way things are in reality.

Yes, we do have an emotional life. We have emotions of concern to the point of "love" in that sense, and we can be angry, upset or frightened (that we have inadvertently broken or badly bent a law of our existence). We can worry about a friend or a person in your world as we worry about you. We have as many or more emotions than yourself, and some you never dreamed of. We do have jealousies, but not to any great extent. We all want to work together for the good of all and the good of your world also. That is our purpose. To work, otherwise, is the same as death to us. We have penalties for misdemeanors; usually we are given some task we do not particularly care for, and which can be a drudgery.

We have said we are not angels; perfection is not one of our attributes. So we do things sometimes that are not altogether acceptable. Only once in a hundred years does anyone dare to commit what could be called an actual crime, and only once in thousands of years does anyone receive the severe penalty to which we are subject if the crime is of such a nature that it is totally unacceptable in any degree whatsoever. That punishment is—I am not sure how to describe it— that our energies are so mixed up it takes us a few hundred years to get ourselves put back together to function as ourselves again and to progress in our work. In other words, we act somewhat as idiots while we are trying to reconstruct ourselves, and that is why you have detected varying degrees of intelligent behavior among us. Some are not yet fully recuperated from this punishment. But they are very few, and they cannot return to the full area of being until they are very close to their normal selves. Some of these explanations are pretty clumsy, but we have the problem of translation plus the fact that the ideas we want to convey have no comparable analogy in your area. We do not want to be too technical at this time; you do not have a technical vocabulary.

We can tell you a little more of our way of being by describing what we can do rather than how we look. You saw or imagined you saw us as shafts or pillars of light. That is exactly as we would look to you, could you actually see us, but it is not at all how we look to ourselves. To us we see each other as patterns of energy, and we recognize each other by the pattern. Each individual or pattern is able to do specific things. One serves as what you would call a psychiatrist or mind doctor; one is what you would call a nature scientist. While we do not see the physical world as you do, we learn about it through other media and know more than you do yourself, yes, or than any of your nature scientists do. We just have never seen them physically until we have been able to do so through your physical eyes and sometimes through the eyes of a few others.

All of us are students or scholars of some type. We are not medical doctors or healers of any kind. That is the department of another co-existent world, the healers. We can have some contact with them, calling upon them for help in certain instances, but we cannot do healing ourselves. We are not artists, musicians nor accomplished in any art. Perhaps we could turn some of our energies in that direction, but we have so much work to do in our own area that we are not much interested in trying. We do love to see works of art and various entertainments through your eyes, because it helps us to understand persons of your area much better and to give us a much more comprehensive picture of the world than working solely with you would do. You cannot be so many places nor display so much activity as we can see for instance on your television. Even your inane movies help us to understand not only what we see, but the persons for whom it was made. We see so many depths of meanings in whatever we are able to view. All is grist to the mill.

We do not have or perceive color as such in our world. We see patterns of vibrations which appear as color to you. This was one of the things you have shown us that gives us the greatest pleasure— we love your flowers and bright birds even more than you do.

We can vaguely see you from our area of being as individual persons, but it takes a great deal of strain and effort, and then what we see is not as you see yourself physically. Again we see patterns or designs of energy. We have not yet learned how to "read" these patterns very efficiently, for we had no way of knowing what the various designs indicated. By seeing through your eyes and having your analysis of things presented to us, we are beginning to work out a real "Earth science" for ourselves. We refer to the physical world you inhabit as the "Earth" area, indicating it to be physical. I do not know how to translate or give to you for translation very exactly what we call our area of the view of the world. We are not superconsciousness or supermind. Our existence is more qualitative than quantitative, though we ourselves are individuals.

We are going to give you a "resume" of our type of activity pertinent to communicating with you and those like you who try to contact us.

We have called ourselves energy essences or existences, and this is true, but we are also more than that. You, yourself, are an energy essence—you would call this "soul"—plus a physical being in a physically manifested world.

We are energy essences or souls who have never been born into the physical world but have developed here in the world that we call, for ourselves, Ardrea. We are also a kind of pre-physical existence. We are not material or physical as you are, but we are something other than pure energy. You would see it as a wave or current of tiny particles that appear to be charged with energy. They would appear to "rain down" like raindrops or again appear in vibrating waves, like heat waves you see on a hot summer day. And once in a while a wispy, vaporish or foggish undulating "string" would float before your eyes.

When you see these, and we know you have, you are very close to seeing us in as close to "physical" manifestation as we can come. If you saw us in actual being, we would appear as columns or pillars of light—or maybe of flame or fire, depending on our emotional state. There have been only a few instances in which this has been possible.

Instead of physical organs and viscera, we have energy patterns that serve the same purpose. We see, hear, speak and touch, but we have no idea of odor or of color in our world. All is black, white and shades of gray. To us grays are beautiful with many subtle variations. No, our world would not be at all acceptable to you without color, art and music and the things you have learned to love there.

We do use tools, instruments and apparatus of various kinds to get work done, just as you do. We do have pens, tablets, amplifying instruments and just about everything you have except transportation vehicles. We move ourselves by imaging ourselves there instantly. Not imagining.

Just as there had to come a time when you would put a man on the moon, so there had to come a time when we could at last communicate with those willing and capable of cooperating with us to develop telepathic skills needed in this communication and to allow us to see into the physical world. For one thing, we had to develop what we call the double graph, and we have not had that too long, just as you have not had rockets too long. We had to develop our own skills, and we had to experiment with everyone from your world who tried to communicate with us, hoping to find those who were capable of being developed to carry on this kind of communication.

Hweig on

Psychic Essences

UFOs

Communication Modes

Intent

Organization

Expectations

CHAPTER TWO

Resume on Psychic Essences

There is no means by which I can verbally translate the appearance of these personalities to you. They are as souls who have never been born, but vastly evolved souls, very sophisticated and very complex. They are very wise with the wisdom of incredible eons of experience. Their efforts in your behalf are many; they are supportive of many of your endeavors, and they serve to guide and protect. You reach them by means of supplication to whatever gods, great or little, that you pray to, for this is their purpose—to aid you in all your activities. You are fortunate indeed to be able to attract the most evolved ones relative to your own evolutionary status.

Actually, to state it more explicitly, it is the purpose of these personalities to help persons on the earth level of being to reach a fuller and more refined understanding of reality. This is not synonymous with truth. Reality is a thing in itself, not the reality of something but reality itself.

They may not impose their ideas or purposes on anyone in your world; they cannot, or more exactly, may not. It is forbidden, for they live by laws so stringent that to disobey one law is the same as death to them. Of course, they are not actually born and do not actually die, but the "death" they suffer is a kind of scrambling of energies, so complete that it would take them what would seem to you to be hundreds of years to get themselves back into functional condition.

Remember they said they can "shrink" time for work purposes only.

They must wait until someone from your world actively seeks them, or seeks someone they think could be them, for sometimes your people do not know precisely whom they seek and are only experimenting to see if "someone is there." The person from your world has to actually ask for someone from some other unknown world to help them understand the many mysteries hidden from your knowledge. They might not say "someone"; they might ask for knowledge of a certain kind.

Too many times such persons seeking information are asking the spirits of the dead to help them. These are not the spirits of the deceased, and if men or women stick to the spirit idea, they can never know these psychic essences as they could be able to present themselves! They must be accepted as actual personalities, not persons. And they do not in the least care what you call them, as long as you get over the idea of calling them Great Grandfather or Uncle Henry. The spirits of the deceased dwell elsewhere and have other things to do for their own purposes.

These are not spirits but souls. They neither eat nor sleep. If their energies become low they rest, but very briefly. It is mostly a matter of disengaging their minds from one piece of work to another.

And they do have minds! To be more exact, they are almost of the same stuff mind is made of.

You have no comprehension of what "mind" is. Yes, we are just hitting the high spots here, and if we seem to go too quickly over some of these facts it is because we fully intend to come back some day and take each one apart and examine it in great detail.

Here we want first to reveal the idea of such a world of psychic essences existing coincident to your own and to state that such personalities are very capable of helping you in all your endeavors if you but believe in them and are willing to accept their help.

If you will recall, some of the great writers in the English language insisted they had interior aid. Robert Louis Stevenson and Rudyard Kipling were two who gave such credit.

We shall continue with the personalities or unborn souls in later pages. Here we want to extend the thought beyond these creatures, for they too are God's creatures even as you and I, and they show you some of the vivid contrasts between your world and theirs.

Have we mentioned color? They see no color, only patterns of vibrations seeable only as undulations of grayish waves. To them gray and all its subtleties are very beautiful, and they have ways of abstracting these tones from any material object and using them in visual orchestrations of gray, as one in your world would create symphonies of sound. This is their only art form, a mode of relaxation. I, myself, do not know how it is possible, for I am only a mere human like yourself! But when I am visiting their world in my purely psychic essence, I can also play with such abstracts, and that is only to play with them; I cannot do the abstracting or orchestrating, nor can I make art of them. They laugh at my efforts and gently refuse to tell me the secrets. They too can tease!

From their world, the people of your world are seen, not in physical form, but as energy patterns. They call these patterns by your name, recognizing the individual. By the constantly complex changes going on in your energy pattern they can tell if you are glad or unhappy and the degree thereof, where you hurt physically, and of course exactly what you are thinking. This is not true telepathy, but it is a direct reading of the mind pattern. When I enter their world in my psychic being, I can do the same, but only with very special sanction that has been denied us for some time. By this method we were formerly able to choose those to help us.

To speak of "being chosen" in this fashion has no spiritual meaning whatever. It is simply a very human person chosen for their life-long attitudes of goodwill, helpfulness and a certain spiritual longing.

Considerable time has been spent in analyzing and then developing a person such as our Ida, toward the purpose of working for us or with us as collaborators, if their understanding and their faith in us is strong enough. We could not accomplish this analysis and long period of development without the aid of the co-existent world, both the opportunities it offers us to work therein and the unsurpassed helpfulness of its own personalities.

Now to a confession I should have made before. Because of misuse by some of our number, we are denied the privilege of reading the minds of earth people even when we are in this psychic world, without first asking sanction of those higher beings who grant it according to our purposes. We must work instead through telepathy in its many variants, but none of which allow us direct access into the thoughts of others without their knowledge. We therefore work through the personages of this world rather than directly with your mind. We should have explained this simply and directly from the first, for this is the reason everything gets so confused and complicated as far as who is concerned. If we zig-zag back and forth between our various facets of being and try to present ourselves both directly and indirectly at the same time, we become confused as well. We hope this explanation clarifies rather than confuses further.

During Ida's first attempts to contact "someone" with her pendulum, her call was answered by these alternate world personalities, or entities, if you like the word, and this was instantly brought to our (UFO personalities') attention, for we had tried many times in many ways to gain her attention. We made the error that first time by leaving too much to the personalities of this psychic world, thinking we could take over when she had reached a certain stage of awareness. Some of the mischievous ones of whom we have told, not malevolently, but teasingly, broke into the serious efforts and caused her great suffering and fear, not knowing how little she realized about them. We knew our mistake too late and since that time have worked diligently to bring her back into a state of usefulness to us. Besides, we have learned to care for and respect a very hard-working, keen-thinking earth human, or more personally put, a plump, jolly woman who makes us all laugh when things are looking most grim and who besides has offered some very acute observations as to better ways of accomplishing our purposes so as not to frighten nor endanger other people on Earth.

Some of our ways in the past have not been too wise or altogether too concerned. We mend our ways. We will have a great deal more to say about contacts and contactees a little later.

We do not mean to tease by always saying we will tell more "later," but there is so much to tell we hardly know which is more important to get across first. We are trying to start with the more simple forms of personalities engaged in this overall, ages-planned-for, tremendous project.

So now whether to go on with this co-existent world showing its inhabitants as the inspirators of your own world, or to go directly into the expose of those like myself? Maybe I am a little too anxious to talk about myself!

Let us go along then with these personalities of your co-existent world that is one of your co-existent worlds, for there are several, and this is the psychic one. In this relationship we shall call them the inspirators.

From the beginning, Man has been helped interiorly. Sometimes he has known it, sometimes suspected it, but most often has been oblivious to it all. He has credited many gods and beings with this interior aid, but only a few have guessed anywhere near the truth or even approximated seeing the reality. Inspiration and sudden illumination have resulted in major works of literature, art, music and all creative endeavors from weaving a basket to chiseling a monument.

A privileged few, by great study and concentration, have managed to peek beyond the obscuring shell between the two worlds. Swedenborg, da Vinci, Bacon and Shakespeare are a few who have known secrets greater than they have ever told. Perhaps this is the time to break through this shell, to amalgamate the efforts of both worlds, so those who care can come into greater creative accomplishment than could be experienced on their own.

Then too, this co-existent world cooperates and collaborates so beautifully with the UFO world. It is another way to synchronize our efforts.

In the past many, many have been helped by the inspirators but then forgot the humbleness with which they began and became blown up with their own importance, and by that time true interior help was all but impossible. The first lesson of all is: relaxation and prayer. Prayer, not to any particular god, just a simple willingness to accept aid and to give thanks for it. Is this so great an offering to those who help? It must be, for few retain it beyond their first one or two successful productions. After that it becomes an ego trip and the inspirators withdraw in disgust. They are not gods or spirits to be propitiated, but they are intelligent existences who work very hard to help and just like to be acknowledged and thanked. And if you wish to say, "Dear God, thank you for all the help and guidance you have given me today," they will understand they are included in your recognition, and they will be pleased.

But there! They have never been so overtly revealed to be either thanked or ignored! So how can they be acknowledged? That is the purpose of including them so thoroughly right here.

Now we will talk about ourselves, the UFO people, and proceed into the exposition of why we were engaged in our psychic essence being and, with the help of the energy existences, in the training of Ida, and of what that training consisted.

Ida declares she notices little difference in herself, but this is because the training has not yet been released into her consciousness. She has complained, more than once, that something "seems to be going on in my sleep, for when I wake suddenly in the night or early morning I hear a conversation or voice going on in my head, and I am not dreaming." This is the manner in which her little head has been filled with all kinds of training and knowledge. It is the same as your psychologists call "sleep learning," but we are using a much more sophisticated form and without her knowledge. Incidentally, we have had to discontinue this for a time, as her mental energies were becoming depleted with 24-hour-a- day bombardment from us. She does not have our capabilities of mental restoration.

The knowledge imparted thus will be released into her consciousness bit by bit as the proper events emerge to make them pertinent and useful.

The first step we took with Ida was to ascertain how deeply religious she might be, and of what her ideas of religious matters consisted. Even there her open-mindedness on one hand, coupled with genuine skepticism of all closed religions on the other hand, proved most responsive to our needs.

"God is whatever you think God is, for God is everything." That was a declaration in a high school essay over sixty years ago, and that is still the basis and total of a firm faith with her. The rest she leaves in the category of "not known for sure." On this basis we have been able to develop in her still unconscious consciousness a deep appreciation of all aspects of Creative being; not created, creative. For all nature is evolving according to its own choices; all things that live have free will. Inanimate objects of nature, or seemingly inanimate, since the word is a misnomer, do not have free will, but nonetheless have "life" of a kind, the life of molecular action. There must be both life and free will for a thing to evolve, and that kind of evolution is actually a continuing or on-going of self-creation. With application of free will the evolution or creation is self-chosen and self-applied. We will not go deeper into the metaphysical aspects at this time.

Ida has said that she saw "life" stirring within the thing as the witness of God being within that thing. And that is all the religion she ever needed to know. Anything else is not only inaccurate but simply window dressing gloss or gilding the lily. (This last is my, Hweig's, observation.)

God is. God is everything. And life is the witness of God within. Yes, and life and spirit are synonymous. That is all the religion one needs to build a very sound and solid understanding of the rest of nature's principles and activities. Would that all men had such a firm and simplistic faith as our Ida!

Over-laden religious concepts are the greatest of all stumbling blocks in our communication with persons in your world. The second is the closed minds, what Ida calls the "cast iron heads." If persons would only listen to us with absolutely open minds, abandoning nothing of their principles or loyalties, but just come willing to listen and think! It would simplify our task beyond measuring.

We are not going any more deeply into a discussion of spiritual or divine matters at this time. What we go on to tell of now is of the psychic nature, not spiritual. There is so much confusion between the two.

We are determined to expose some of the miscalculations and misconceptions of your people, and thereby we will find many in opposition to what we say. We know this, but we can no more than say it, for it is the truth!

Man, in his dawning, was a simple soul. His simple needs and desires were offset, however, by terrible fears. And from these fears rose all the mishaps, dishonors, tragedy and pain suffered ever since.

Fear is the bugaboo of human existence. All your pain, suffering and disease rise from elements of fear, not evil. Fear is the force that destroys human happiness, health, welfare and all good things.

In Ida we had to work mightily to eradicate some very deep and long-held fears, and our task is not yet done.

The greatest fear of all is the fear of loss! One can even fear to lose that which he does not have, but which he only hopes to have, or which he hopes his children or his people may have. Or he may fear to lose something he does not actually possess but which he believes should be in a certain place or certain way.

So the elemental man, the earliest man, feared loss just as deeply, as poignantly and as violently as modem man. And from this fear of loss rose all the wrong doing, all the human evil of the world. We are going to get some mighty arguments about this!

But, using Ida as an example, we show how we have tried to combat her fears. Her greatest fear has always been the fear of doing something "wrong," although she found it all but impossible to find a solid basis on which to judge right or wrong.

Always Ida has been most fearful of doing something she "shouldn't," something to be chided for, just some silly mistake or to "make an ass of herself." It has held her back from many things she might have done! And in some instances, this has been not altogether a bad thing, for she does have a tendency to go barging into things without overmuch thought or preparation. Fortunately for us, or she never would have taken up the pendulum.

We tried to combat her fears in the following ways: First, by making her recapitulate all her mistakes and self-judged crimes. She complained that she spent at least two years, several years back, with her mind constantly running over and over all the mistakes she had made in her life. Ida could not know we were impelling this. One by one she took them up, faced them, confessed them, analyzed them in the light of her latest knowledge and discovered they were not that bad after all. We helped in the analysis, in the self-consultation and in the conclusions. We did have great and serious sanction to do this. When this episode was over, Ida was more free and easy in her mind than she had ever been. We were preparing her for this new era in her life in which she could write for us without any weight of uncertainty about herself or any weight of guilt. Actually the things that disturbed her most were silly little awkward errors, social mostly, when she felt horribly gauche and stupid.

Next to her fear of wrongdoing is the fear of appearing stupid, and that she has never been. Ignorant, unfortunately so, but stupidity is not one of her traits.

So ignorance was another task we worked on for more years than she knows. How to impel her to overcome some of the blank spots in her knowledge? That would take a volume to explore; we can only give a quick summation. She is an avid reader, though her retention is not too good. She reads too fast, for one thing, "skimming the cream," she calls it. And here is something that exasperates me beyond words; she reads everything from back to front. Every time she takes up a new book I grit my teeth to keep from speaking out, and it is not in my jurisdiction to criticize her mannerisms. Of course she says she wants to know what a book is aiming at before she bothers to read it, and the conclusions are always on the last few pages. But does she have to read the whole blooming thing from back to front. All right, Ida dear, I said I would tell on you, now go on typing please.

Perhaps it is our fault that she reads so fast and does not retain everything, for we have not wanted her to get bogged down in some study not useful to our purpose. At the same time we wanted to extend her range of knowledge in many areas and ways. She has managed to get a wide variety of facts at her fingertips and a 23-year session as proprietor of several antique stores has broadened her view of many kinds of art and artifacts. Considerable travel has shown her the contents of many major museums of the world, which is quite a broad area of information. But always her main interest has been the study of people, how they live, act, feel and why.

Through the influence of her husband, she had dipped into some of the scientific thought of the day and has learned something of the economic problems of her world. Politics leaves her cold, but the present sociological problems on Earth have her deeply distressed, if not very well informed.

Bit by bit she broadened the areas of her knowledge, never guessing how much she was being influenced and guided by us, the UFO people, always with the patient help and gentle care of the inspirators.

From the day of her birth, Ida has been the protege of the one who first introduced himself as "the Nameless One." Someone took over that name, and in order not to be confused with that second one, we have now given the Guardian the name of "The Hidden One." Someday this mystery will also be clearly revealed, but not for the passage of some time.

The Hidden One carefully guided and guarded Ida through the aid of the inspirators who make the direct contacts, just as they made contact for us in the beginning of the pendulum episode.

We have given but a glimpse of the co-existent world of psychic existences in which we are sometimes active inhabitants, but we shall have much more to tell later of our other areas of being and much else concerning the UFO world and its allies.

Persons contacted and developed in this unseen, unguessed way by us have all been chosen years ago and they are waiting, without knowing, for our call to come forth. Soon all will be uncovered. Some have been prematurely disclosed mainly through psychological accidents. Their revelations remain as great mysteries, but only for a short time. All will be explained.

Now I get to talk about myself, Hweig, and my sturdy colleagues Amorto and Jamie, and to tell you how we came to first "meet" our Ida.

Amorto, Jamie, and I, Hweig, came from our physical world aboard a UFO, one of the hardware kind, in your year 1940.

Ida was traveling with her first husband and two other men in a car on the desert between Indio and Blythe. As they came over a hill the valley before them was crimson, as though with fire, and they immediately thought of a forest fire, but could see no flames. Ida did indeed witness the UFO that brought Amorto, Jamie and me to earth, and that is where we first "met" her. We firmly believe, but cannot at this time prove, that this meeting was planned and engineered, probably by The Hidden One.

Our craft that night had many sophisticated instruments, one of them a scanner that allowed us to "see" the car and its occupants. We observed the three men and Ida and tried to speak telepathically to all of them. The two men had been too well brainwashed to receive us. Her husband was not in a mental accord to receive us. Only Ida was, and we made her forget what she heard and saw that night. And this is what I said to her.

"Do not be alarmed. We come as friends. Someday I shall speak to you again. Wait for me and expect me."

But I was told this contact was premature, and I must erase it from her mind, which I did. But perhaps not from her subconscious, for she has said that years later she would find herself looking from her window and "grieving" and saying to herself, "Why am I grieving? I've not lost anyone. I am perfectly happy. Why do I grieve?"

And Ida and I have decided between us that perhaps the memory of my words that night were somehow making their way into her emotions, if not thoughts. Or am I too presumptuous to say she was grieving for me? But she has said that since our first telepathic contact with her in 1968 that she has never had that feeling of grief again. Oh well, I do presume too much!

Hweig

CHAPTER THREE

Hallucinatory Events

We, the people of the UFOs speak to the respected inhabitants of Planet Earth to explain the methods we have used to make contact with them.

Due to our lack of knowledge of the Earth people, to our haste in trying to make contacts and to the fear and sometimes aggressiveness with which we were met, we have made many errors. We ask for leniency of judgment until we have had the opportunity to present ourselves in a more circumspect manner.

Through a correspondent we have found adaptable to our needs, talented and willing to intercede in our behalf, we offer this series of explanations of our acts and intentions.

We have meant no harm to anyone, and incidences of this nature distress us far more than the recipient.

Through the help of your scientists we hope to explain much, but to the general populace we have even more to tell.

First, let us speak of the manner or manners in which we are seen or otherwise make ourselves known:

1. Actual physical craft and human or humanoid (as you call them) occupants are seen or encountered.

2. Hallucinatory craft and occupants due to the hypnosis of the contactees.

3. Craft/personalities are unseen, but their presence detected. These are psychic manifestations.

4. Remote contact by telepathy and other means, mostly mechanical.

5. More immediate and personal contacts by means we cannot reveal at this time.

In this story we want to reveal our uses of hallucinatory events.

1. We use hallucination for one type of contactee only:

    a. Must be fairly young.

      b.   Must have strong religious background.

      c.   Must be alerted to such phenomena through news stories or

           other media.

      d.   Must have considerable respect for authority fig-ures.

      e.   Must be willing to sacrifice own desires for responsible purposes.

      f.   Must be alert to circumstances, observant and curious.

2.   We choose contactees long in advance; no contact is accidental.

3.   We choose illusory experiences to fit the contactee.

4.   Our intentions are for the contactee to come forward at certain times in the future, with acknowledgment of the incident. Sometimes, due to psychological accidents, they remember too soon.

Therefore, we want to reassure these contactees by the following:

1.   Soon you will understand why this incident occurred and what it is to mean to your future.

2.   No harm will come to you or your people.

3.   Future events are timed to coincide with the purpose of your contact. Be patient.

4.   Many besides yourself await the timed event. You are not alone. Most of them do not now remember; they are timed to remember.

5.   Certain powerful forces will be available for your use when the time is ready.

6.   You will be able to do something remarkable and very worth-while because of your contact.

We have told of the psychic manifestation, those in which we visit the Earth in what you call "out-of-body" experiences. At such times we make apparent craft seemingly appear and disappear in a twinkling, even out of the sea!

Remember, at all times our intentions are beneficial and our desires peaceable.

Hweig

CHAPTER FOUR

Psychic Manifestations

We have given you some explanations concerning the manner in which, and the reasons why, we use manifestations of a psychic nature. (See Part II, Chapter 1.)

Now, lest all this alarm you unduly, we must add:

We cannot do all this idly or for our personal purposes or amusement. Laws governing our actions are most stringent. To use these abilities in your world requires special sanctions for use on specific occasions only.

Our purpose in coming in this invisible state is to establish communication with as many earth persons as possible, to develop telepathic contacts with those capable and to find out for ourselves what we can of the nature and ways of Earth beings. Our abilities in this state are greatly limited. We do not find it the most productive method of making contacts or gaining information.

The energies we use to do these things are as available to you as they are to us. You will be taught to use them.

We too look to higher forces for guidance, and our punishment is swift and inevitable if we use our powers arbitrarily or for unsanctioned purposes.

We *are part of a great plan. We are sent to inform and make aware. We are helpers of the universe.*

Hweig

CHAPTER FIVE

Remote Contact and Telepathy

Dear People of the Planet Earth:

We must tell you now of the manner in which we make telepathic contact with those of your inhabitants who are able to receive us, such as Ida, who transcribes these writings for me.

First, the communicant must be introduced into a psychic dimension through your so-called hypnosis or trance. In this case the hypnosis was self-induced, as though by accident.

The psychic dimension is a world co-existent to your own, existing in the same space, but in a different time dimension. All psychic phenomena transpires with the aid of psychic existences who partake of these dimensions. In our out-of- body experiences we too can partake of time potentials of this world co-existent in the same space as yourself. At present, in these short pages I cannot make this more clear.

The psychic existences of this co-existent world act as a go-between for our telepathic messages. These existences are of several classes or complexities. The most developed are those who are very much like souls who have never been born into a physical world. They are very, very wise, with eons of wisdom and are dedicated to aiding those of your world who actively seek their assistance.

Once we were alerted by these existences that Ida was ready to receive telepathy, our part was to reach through them by their abilities to activate a certain gland that lies low in the brain, unknown to you and undiscoverable by scalpel or x-ray. Only through use can it be discovered. We activated this gland through the services of the psychic existences and thereafter began a long process of development of her telepathic abilities. Sometimes through physical accident, this gland is activated in certain others.

At first we reached our lady from our out-of-body state and from close by her side. She would have fainted to know how close. (But we do not, and cannot, invade interiorly.)

After her abilities to receive and send were well developed, we no longer needed the services of our psychic existence friends, but could transmit and receive directly to and from her. She became fluent very rapidly. Then we were able to return to our own place of being and the very close contact was no longer necessary.

This is something your researchers are just now learning, that distance, to a telepathic communicant well developed, makes no difference whatever. The moon, the stars, the sun, our own planet, which is a long piece away, no distance is too great for well-developed telepathic communicants.

We can deliver our messages by two methods. The receiver can either

1. Hear the actual physical vibration as though a voice were speaking in his ear, or

2. A movement of meaning or words can be received in the mind without physical vibrations.

It is almost as though one were talking to oneself. In this particular case we use the second method and allow the words to become apparent to Ida in tones very much, though not altogether, like her own.

We tried the first method with her in 1968 on our first contact and only succeeded in scaring her half to death.

On our second attempt we used the second method and found her extremely capable and facile in telepathic writing, which she is now using to receive and transmit to you these essays.

If we used our own tones of speech, the alien sound might frighten her again!

We do not mean to insinuate that Ida is in any way timid! She could not possibly know what was happening to her, and we had no way of explaining until her abilities were well developed. Could we make her understand in time, before she panicked and left? That was always the uppermost question.

We are now working with many other people on your planet, trying to establish telepathic communication. Because of our success with this correspondent and the things she has taught us, we are having greater and greater success with our other contacts.

To us, you are the alien forms, and we have had to learn you in many ways. Even though we came originally from a common source, eons and eons separate our beginnings until now, and certain evolutionary differences as well as the total difference of our lifehoods gave us no clue what to expect in contacting your people.

We have made grave errors. We receive general instructions from higher sources. We plan specifics to carry out these instructions. We have come to believe we are being taught as much or more than we intended to teach you!

Hweig

CHAPTER SIX

Remote Contact and Laser Beams

People of Planet Earth:

In this writing we wish to tell you of things our collaborator here knows nothing about. Laser beams are a deep mystery to her.

Your own world has discovered the beam, in a one-sided sort of way, but has no knowledge of its many uses, particularly as a means of remote scanning.

We will give no scientific data at this time, but we will tell you how we use it, why it works and what we hope to accomplish through its use in the future.

The laser beam we use is a full beam, not at all the one-sided affair you have discovered. However, you will soon receive more information. You must learn some disadvantages and dangers of its use first. In another writing we shall tell of this, but through a different correspondent. Ida here works on psychic matters only.

In one aspect the use of the laser beam conjoins with psychic forces and then is used as a scanner, by which we can see into your world in a multitude of ways.

Here again the laws by which we live do not permit us to use the beam for discovering governmental or military secrets, or for intimate personal matters.

We can, however, scan your industrial plants, financial institutions and political and religious establishments in all their public aspects. Professional or sacred secrets are barred to us. By the wariness and interference of other dedicated personalities, our laser beam is rendered impotent in such cases; the psychic aid is withdrawn, and we are powerless to pry.

By use of our laser scanner we can pick up and inspect the life activities of those we wish to consider as contactees. Many are considered, but few are able to complete total development. The lives of our actual contactees must be dedicated to service and to supervising the welfare and happiness of others, or must be those persons who by obvious traits and observable actions will develop into personalities of such a nature. We can tell by the age of five if a person is so aimed, and we can begin a life-long, though intermittent scan, at that age. Checking in occasionally to see the actual development of our potential contactee, we can by devious but not harmful means, nudge that person in the direction of certain studies and activities we wish them to follow.

Sometimes other influences pull the contactee into other paths. We mourn then, and strive to bring them back to our purposes, but frequently the actual pull of the world is too strong for us to counteract, for we work from great, and sometimes even greater distances and without the power of actual physical contact.

We have found that too close use of the laser beam is imprudent because the people of Earth do not have the necessary protective pigments. Your native American Indians have the most protective skins. This does not mean you have to be "red" men, for we certainly are not! But the copper colored pigment is Earth's best substitute for the actually colorless pigment which protects fully from the laser beam.

The American Indians, among other so-called primitive peoples, have great psychic abilities. We have had varied contacts with them over many centuries, but their knowledge of us was obscured by their ideas of spiritual forces. Among all the people at present on Earth, the Indian has the closest relationship to our past. This is purposely an enigmatic statement.

We were not aware of the differences in skin pigments, and thereby some Earth people suffered from too close exposure. Only after taking many skin samples from all over the world, could we analyze and understand the qualities of skin tissue which allowed the burning sensation, and which of the Earth people could stand the beam best, and even then, not perfectly. We have learned to shield its full power.

We have many mistakes to answer for, but this overall work is so vital to the peace and continuance of your world that we must work as best we can to accomplish our tasks.

Our *purpose is mutual cooperation, understanding and accomplishment. We need your help. You need ours!*

Hweig

CHAPTER SEVEN

Electromagnetic Impulses

Dear People of Earth:

Again I come to tell you of another manner of contact with the Planet Earth.

Electromagnetic impulses are of myriad kinds. Mind activity depends on them, but this is only one.

We use a very subtle form of electromagnetic energies, complementary to mind, but not analogous. It is still much different from telepathy.

This is the most difficult matter I have to try to describe to you, for your basis of knowledge is too small. I have so little to build on.

These energies are a part of physical nature, but on the borderline of psychic manifestation, a kind of no man's land between the two where it can be utilized either physically or psychically. Actually the psychic nature of man devotes itself to the uses of physical man. I fear that is clumsy, but how better can I say it now? Later, after much more information on all these subjects has been imparted, this will become more clear.

These energies are delivered to the human brain as impulses or impulsions (to distinguish them from the acts of impulsive people).

The impulsions delivered stimulate responsive vibrations in the brain which enforce certain activities of the individual.

Without quite knowing why, he may arise, go to the door, open it, and then wonder why he is doing it. He cannot remember if he had a purpose or not. He did not. We did.

No, we do not in any way control the actions of Earth persons. We stimulate, through the use of these impulsions of an electromagnetic nature, the impetus to action on the part of the individual. We cannot enforce obedience. We can never tamper with free will. But in this manner we suggest an action we wish to see accomplished.

The types of actions and the purposes thereof are many indeed.

We may want to observe a person, who, for some physical reason, cannot be reached by our scanner. We then, through impulsions, cause him to go out in the open, the street or his backyard, wherever we may observe him better.

Sometimes we need to know something contained in a certain book or magazine, and because of the electromagnetic impulses, the impulsions, we cause him to consider buying, borrowing or somehow reading this item. We can then kibitz over his shoulder in our own inimitable fashion and "read" for ourselves. In such a case the reading is combined with a sort of recording, not a camera but like that, and we thereafter have the book for our own use.

The impulsions combine readily with certain psychic abilities by which we are able to produce some fantastic results.

By these methods we can make sure a person is in the right place at the right time to observe our craft and/or occupants. We can make sure he obtains a basic knowledge necessary to understand things that are to come in his future. By these means we can reach him and extend his knowledge through sleep learning, which we shall tell of at another time.

We can cause certain operations of machinery to fail or certain well-conceived plans to fall flat, so many things we cannot begin to speak of them in so short a treatise. Our lady will write much more voluminously in the future on these subjects.

So much to tell! And our time allowance is not forever!

In no way can we control the minds or the activities of Earth persons. In some few extreme instances, in matters of vital concern, we impel with great force, but we cannot compel.

Our contactees are never mind controlled.

All of our contactees have better health, happier lives and longer ones because of our concern and interest in them.

We, the people of the UFOs have been questioned by your media concerning many things.

We *have nothing to do with the cattle mutilations. We have nothing to do with the men in black. We have nothing to do with tragic accidents to self or families. We work very, very hard to accomplish beneficial tasks. Thousands of times we have led our contactees into helpful paths and conditions. Our task is to aid in the evolution of Man on the planet Earth.*

Hweig

CHAPTER EIGHT

Sleep Learning

To the People of Planet Earth:

Once Ida complained that when she woke suddenly in the night or early morning, she could hear a "voice" running on in her mind that stopped abruptly as she awoke. She was positive it was something other than a dream.

Quite so. It was my own voice she heard, reading endless information to her as she slept. Not all night, of course, for I too must sleep, though very little.

In this manner we reach many of our contactees, even those who cannot receive direct telepathy. We use the combined instrumental devices utilizing electromagnetic impulsions and a certain psychic phenomenon unknown as yet to you of the Earth.

We are in doubt as to the number of persons who are alerted to the reception of this sleep learning, a method of imparting valuable secrets that has been used for nearly 50 years and for several thousand of our contacts. In this manner we can prepare them for eventful times ahead. The information is timed to appear in consciousness when most needed to meet some coming pressures and stresses. They are prepared to do many useful, beneficial and wise things of which they now have no waking knowledge.

This stratum of information cannot be reached through your variety of hypnosis, nor by any other means at your command.

We must hasten to make clear that:

1. All information is valuable and beneficial.
2. No one's mind has ever been tampered with.
3. The learning experience has no dire consequences to the person receiving, except that in a few rare cases there may be a feeling of tiredness in the morning. It will quickly disperse.

4. The understanding of the knowledge given may not be present in the person at the time of the giving. Therefore it is timed to become known when the proper conjunction of events takes place in that person's future.

5. Not all information comes "through" at once, but may emerge over many months or years.

6. The knowledge given is in line with a person's highest ambitions, hopes, and personal desires.

There need be no concern that the information is other than good, beneficial and in the best interests of the recipient.

All over the world men and women are suddenly finding that answers to long-standing and severe problems come to surface with a suddenness and ease that is almost shocking. New cures, new methods of pain relief or new ideas for making the world a healthier and happier place are ideas that just come out of the blue? No indeed, just out of that person's sleep learning prompted by the people of the UFOs.

Can we prove this? We can say it most easily, but how can we prove it?

By telling a few things that will be found in the near future, not because we are prognosticators, but because the sleep learners are timed for the information to come forth.

1. A cure for diabetes involving electrical treatment.

2. Control of epilepsy without drugs.

3. The understanding of so-called schizophrenia that will allow complete rearrangement of the sufferer's mental abilities—in effect, a permanent cure.

We know these things will happen because we have given the necessary information. Until then:

Be not fearful. We come as friends. We seek to collaborate with those who wish to benefit all mankind.

Hweig

CHAPTER NINE

Observable Craft

People of Planet Earth:

In the past, many of our physical craft have been observed, but even more hallucinatory craft were apparent. It is most difficult to distinguish one from the other by sight or vision alone.

This is a matter and condition that will require in-depth explanation later, when time and wordage permit. For you of Earth, who do not deal in semi-corporeal states, it is difficult to understand or imagine the degree of reality and the degree of illusion as they meet in this semi-corporeal state of man and craft. They are real, but not physical, capable of interaction, but not of physical contact.

As for bases under the sea, they do indeed exist, but in a strange manner that we cannot take time to touch on here. They are not bases for physical or hardware craft, but have a purpose and use for the semi-corporeal or illusory state. Hard to imagine? Even more difficult to describe!

For now this must suffice concerning observable craft. You have been given a few hints useful to separate the real from the illusion.

The day of deliberate confusion is ended. Our future approaches will deal in realities. How can we come as friends if you do not know what we are and what we are not?

Hweig

CHAPTER TEN

Observable Occupants

To the People of Planet Earth:

We may say here that the illusionary beings can be given any form and often are created to match certain expectations in the con- tactee's mind. Our experiences in use of these pure illusions are not at all satisfactory and produce nothing but distress and fear. Their use is, therefore, being stringently curtailed.

On our home planet our "natives" are strictly as human as yourselves, with a few minor evolutionary differences. We came from the same roots.

As workers and helpers we have many other types of beings, some of them extremely odd or even weird to your understanding. We have learned not to use those that seem to scare the hell out of your people. At first we did not know they were so completely for- eign to your knowledge.

The workers we now use are from another planetary system even further from Earth than we are. They have no connection with the race of humans on Earth or with us. They are, however, highly intelligent and vastly knowledgeable in many sciences and crafts. Their collaboration is indispensable to this endeavor, so please, dear people of Earth, try to accept them respectfully in all their peculiari- ties. They are stiff and formal in mannerisms, but truly compassion- ate and benign.

Our humans, comparable to yourselves, are all of the scientific and scientific-engineering class. Few of us ever leave the home plan- et bodily.

We are also bonded with other planetary peoples in various re- lationships, some of whom are navigators on the physical craft.

This is as far as we want to go into the matter of ourselves and our colleagues at the present time. There is much to be told, and in time it shall be.

We are trying in this series to give a comprehensive view of ourselves and our approaches to Earth.

Our understanding of Earth problems becomes more specific and detailed daily. We are here to help develop qualities and to give knowledge that will help you cope with such problems, not as specific plans for each detailed problem, but as a great development of abilities and extensions of powers, which will become instrumental in solving your vast complex of troubles.

We are not superhuman, nor are we dolts. We come to share our knowledge and our powers so you may help yourselves in all ways.

Hweig

CHAPTER ELEVEN

Purposes and Intent

Dear People of Earth:

The plan for Project Earth was given to us more than a century ago. We have worked for many years to break the greater plan down into smaller components so that we might advance on many small fronts simultaneously.

The Great Plan is not ours, nor are we the only ones engaged in the instrumenting of it. Others besides ourselves are working as feverishly, and in our next essay we shall reveal some of these.

For ourselves, our tasks and our problems are many. We have come to believe we are being given a training program and lessons in many things such as human relationships at the same time.

Our part of the Great Plan is to help the Earth humans evolve a step higher in the scale of development allotted to them, and the next step is the one of psychic or soul development. Soul is not spiritual, spirit is. Soul and psyche are just that, psychic, and that is where we are masters. Also we are to help the Earth people advance in the physical applications of science and in technology, in which we are far advanced.

Many secrets have been imparted through sleep learning and through other devices in the past fifty years, but not enough. Our successful contacts are too few, and the time is at hand when much more rapid progress is needed and will be even more needed very soon.

Therefore we are now ready for person-to-person contacts through telepathy and even direct communications. We find, however, that we have hampered our own endeavors by some very foolish moves. Our idea of protective covering at first was to keep the people of Earth completely confused as to our actual being and purposes. The kickback from this major stupidity has been horrendous. Not knowing what type of persons the Earth people had become, and viewing through scanners some of the terrible activities that take place on Earth today, we did not know of the thousands of honorable and decent and compassionate people who dwell in the midst of so much corruption, crime, disease, famine and war. Such a pall of violence and horror lies over the Earth! To find the good in so much bad was like finding your proverbial needle in a haystack.

But it is there! And there in great quantity, though timidly hidden beneath fears and concerns and worried brows of those who become faint-hearted at the possibility of making any kind of a dent in the shield of evil that lies over the Earth.

It can be done. We have come to help, not to preach.

We have cures and medical processes for nearly every physical disease, and psychic knowledge for every illness of the soul, and technological and scientific advances for every mechanical need.

This is the extent of our aid, but others shall come forth at the proper time with guidance of other natures. There are even those who can help in the economic distress that mounts hourly throughout the world.

Our part in the Great Plan is not necessarily the largest part, but it is the first to declare itself openly, and to plead for the acceptance of friendship and the collaboration of our Earth associates to make your planet a saner and more logical place of abode.

So many good people have already placed themselves at our disposal. The more who come to realize what we are trying to do, the more acquiesce to our pleas for friendship.

Nothing can be done to you individually or collectively against your free will. Somehow there has always been some kind of agreement to our plea, even though it was a subconscious one. This is too deep a subject to go into here.

The rules under which we work are the most stringent in existence. We dare not break one, and indeed none of us want to, for collaborating in the Project Earth program is the greatest adventure of all time, for us, and we hope for you too!

We are not alone. Others await also. The total plan is rejuvenation of the Earth and its people.

Hweig

CHAPTER TWELVE

Total Organization

We have come to the point at long last where we may reveal certain events and happenings behind the scenes that will help you understand what is going on.

To begin with, this plan is so huge that it cannot all be completed and experienced in a millennium. But already much has occurred in a half-realized sort of way.

Explanations are difficult because of your lack of basic facts.

1. The study of psychic phenomena will soon be based upon an exact and provable science. Already certain ones have been given outlines of study and valuable information.

2. Problems involving great economic turmoil are being considered, and answers given are slowly seeping into the conscious awareness of very influential persons. A whole new science of economics is about to be uncovered, not delivered by the UFO people, but by our allies.

3. Many medical and health problems are in the process of being solved, some by UFO information, others by personalities from other sources. We cannot now be more explicit, but such sources exist.

4. Racial problems are going to come into a new understanding. One faction of our allies is working industriously on this problem alone. Relief is close.

5. Another faction that works with us, but not of UFO origin, is developing certain Earth persons in those abilities that will allow great natural sources of power to become known and utilized. The days of coal power and oil power are numbered, and fewer than you think. Presently unknown sources of energy will be discovered.

6. Other allied sources are working on more obscure problems involving population distribution and living necessities for the

billions of people on Earth. An end to poverty and disease can and must be a reality, without the burden falling on the hard-working, industrious and responsibility-assuming persons.

7.   The first and major move will be against crime and violence. Your cities are to become places of beauty and quietude. Do not laugh at that choice of words—quietude is what we said and mean.

All of this cannot be accomplished in the twinkling of an eye or by the waving of a magic wand. It must come through the dedicated efforts of the thinking people of Earth and a great deal of hard work, intensive thought, acquiescence to both outer and inner help and with some groaning and travail. Nothing so vital can be easy.

Complete rejuvenation of the inner person comes first. It will happen more quickly than you believe possible. From there the outer rejuvenation of his surroundings becomes inevitable.

The unseen helpers are myriad. It is too soon to unveil all their secrets, but one by one these are being told, and the answers to all mysteries discovered.

The total organization is so vast that the number of personalities working therein is staggering and unimaginable. Centuries have been spent in the preliminaries, the breaking down of the overall plan into manageable segments and the learning of their appointed tasks by the participants. As conditions change on Earth, plans have had to be reconstructed, until they become flexible from minute to minute. If we tell one thing one day too decisively we have to retract or change it the next due to changes in the overall circumstances. This sets us up as untrustworthy and liars.

Forgive us then for not being too explicit herein. What we write now may change within the hour, due to the untellable enormity of the whole event.

Be assured that the work is being planned and carried on by thousands and thousands and thousands of souls, each with his bit to impart or teach, some from the UFO worlds, but even more from other worlds, and worlds within worlds of which you have no present concept.

Eventually all will be told. The pressure of time is increasing.

We are not moralistic pundits trying to save you from your sins. We are performing a task we have been given: communication, making personal contacts and imparting basic information.

We have worked in other places other times and found certain maneuvers valuable. On Earth these were out of place. They not only did not work for us, they worked against us.

Now, due to the help of certain Earth persons willing to stick their necks out for us and for you, we have come to a better understanding, and we have learned more helpful ways in making contacts.

Have no fear. You are always in full control of your mind and your powers. Nothing can be done to you that you would not have done.

Hweig

CHAPTER THIRTEEN

Future Expectations

In the beginning of this endeavor, our time schedule was quite relaxed, and we felt no pressure. As time goes on we begin to feel a real strain to get on with it more and more quickly.

Certain events coming upon the world, inevitably unless stopped, are already making themselves apparent and more forcibly drawing our attention to the need for some haste.

This is why we are going all out at this time to bring ourselves to your attention through such writings as this and through books and papers for scientific study. The time is now.

You may expect more and more contactees to come forward in the immediate future with understandable stories of their experiences.

Much will be given in such ways as this to aid in the interpretations of past contacts, many of which became known prematurely through various mishaps. As quickly as possible all mysterious events will be explained.

Due to haste and ignorance, some harmful results have occurred. These will be alleviated and compensated for to the best of our abilities. We grieve for such misadventures.

Again, not all of the accidents were our fault by any judgment. Too often the contactee did not listen to instructions and advice and turned against himself in panic or self-interest. We cannot accept responsibility for this.

Because of past incidents we have curtailed certain plans for the future and will use more workable and less obnoxious means of accomplishing certain work. There will be no more "abductions" so-called, for all "abductions" in the past were consented to in one way or another.

A few who by their own free will wanted to adventure to our place of being are now ready to return home. In due time they shall return, not immediately, but presently. They are not many, for all "abductions" laid onto to us were not so. How easy to explain any disappearance as an UFO abduction, and for how many self-conceived reasons!

By our secrecy, we have laid ourselves open to blame for many things we had nothing to do with! Unfortunately for us, we could not be more open until we knew exactly what type of beings we had to contact.

Now for the big and last question we can answer in these pages:

Are we going to invade the Earth forcibly, violently, aggressively, or in any manner whatever? *No.*

We have no military might. We have means of self-defense, rays, radiation and psychic abilities. We do not want your planet. We have more territories and resources than we can ever use, a billion times more. We do not want your people. What, for God's sake, would we do with them? Do we want to take on for ourselves the total problem of housing, feeding, clothing and educating a few billion people?

Deliver us from such problems! We have all the workers and helpers we can use, and with more knowledge, talents and abilities than Earth people now possess. We shudder at such a burden and responsibilities!

We do have problems the Earth people can help us solve, to be told another day. We have learned valuable lessons from our contacts with Earth, lessons we needed to learn.

We do want to come in small numbers in our physical craft and our physical selves to converse, plan and explain openly to your representatives, but this may be a long time in the future. Mutual understanding and trust must be solidly cemented first, so there are no errors or mishaps at the confrontation. We shall come only on the invitation of your representative authorities. Why should we take a chance of getting pulverized by your mighty weapons? An interplanetary war is not desirable for any of us.

We do come from a far planet. We are not crawling out of some loathsome hidden hole on Earth, although there are places on Earth you know not of.

All shall be told another day.

Great mysteries are to be solved.

Great benefits for all mankind are to accrue.

Great good wishes to the people of planet Earth from the people of the UFOs.

Will there be mind invasion by UFOs? In order not to alarm those thinking persons who feel our "invasion" of Earth people's minds is a form of mind control, we would like to point out some salient facts:

1.   At no time is the person forced to act upon our suggestions.

2.   While he cannot "throw off our voices by his own will, he can supplicate whatever gods he appeals to, and we shall withdraw if his intentions are reasonable and consistent with facts. If not, we dally a little to allow us some time to quiet his fears and convince him of our integrity and worth.

3.   If we see that he is too panic-stricken, or not readily able to accept us and our purposes, we withdraw, sometimes temporarily, sometimes permanently.

4.   No matter what the outcome of each mind contact, whether he allows us to stay or insists on withdrawal, his life is carefully monitored thereafter, and as soon as his panic dies down so interaction is possible, he is somehow compensated for his trials, though he never realizes who has brought him such "amazingly good luck."

5.   Everything we say can be and will be verified as fast as the way of doing so can be worked out. We need more willing and dedicated workers on the Earth side. So few have too much to do to get it all done immediately. First things, vital things, must be first, always.

6.   Those who accept us and work for us, though sometimes with great and loud complaints, may be certain that they are doing a great and beneficial thing for their world. Soon there will be hard evidence to prove this.

7.   The practice of mind control by Earth people themselves is far more virulent and effective than anything we could devise. It has been utilized for centuries for all sorts of purposes large and small. It consists of many false proclamations and the steady control of beliefs that enter into every phase of the daily life of Earth man. This is not the form of mind control you are fearful of in our mind invasion, but it is a powerful and destroying force just the same.

Now the great question: How dare we invade Earth minds to the extent that we have? Every mind we have in any way entered acquiesced to this use before that person appeared bodily on Earth.

Reincarnation is a fact.   Pre-birth induction into the ranks of our workers is an absolute necessity before we can engage that person, in his present Earth life, in our purposes. This fact can be verified not only through the proper use of whole hypnosis, but also in other manners that he may use for himself:

a. Sleep memory.

b. Out of body travel.

c. Mind travel (different from b.).

d. A very deep meditation which only those of Master Yoga training or comparable training can attain.

We do not advise that any of these methods be tried without well trained guides or teachers. At present these are almost non-existent, but as quickly as possible information and training shall be brought forward and accomplished. Everything should progress very rapidly, now that we have had this breakthrough in communication.

Be at ease. Above all be patient. Every minute of your night and day we are working feverishly to put all of these plans into operation.

The first of your communication receivers necessarily bear the brunt of hardship and anguish, breaking a path for others to follow. Be patient with them also. Each has his or her own task. Be content to wait a little before judging either them...or us!

Hweig

Resources

and

Bibliography

The Dr. R. Leo Sprinkle Collection

Sprinkle, R. L. "Psychological Implications in the Investigation of UFO Reports," *Flying Saucer Occupants.* L.J. & C.E. Lorenzen, New York, NY: Signet, 1967, 160-186.

___"Personal Views of UFO Investigation." *Symposium on Unidentified Flying Objects,* July 29, 1968, Hearings before the U.S. House Committee on Science and Astronautics, No. 7, Clearing House for Federal Scientific and Technical Information, 5285 Port Royal Road, Springfield, VA 22151, 206-210.

___"Personal and Scientific Attitudes: A Study of Persons Interested in UFO Reports," *Flying Saucer Review,* Special Issue No. 2, June, 1969, 6-10.

___"Some Uses of Hypnosis in UFO Research," *Flying Saucer Review,* Special Issue No. 3, September, 1969, 17-19.

___"Status Inconsistency Theory and Flying Saucer Sightings: A Review," *APRO Bulletin,* Jan/Feb 1971, 4-7.

___"UFO Research: Problem or Predicament?" *Proceedings of MUFON Symposium,* July 1975, 103 Old Towne Road, Sequin, TX 78155, 37-49.

___"A Preliminary Report on the Investigation of an Alleged UFO Occupant Encounter," *Flying Saucer Review,* XXI (1975), Nos. 3 & 4, 3-5.

___"Hypnotic and Psychic Implications in the Investigation of UFO Reports," *Encounters with UFO Occupants,* by C.E. Lorenzen & J. Lorenzen, New York, NY: Berkeley Press, 1976, 256-329.

___"UFO activity: Cosmic Consciousness Conditioning?" *UFO Phenomena,* Bologna, Italy: EDITECS, I (1976), No. 1, 56-62.

___"Hypnotic Time Regression Procedures in the Investigation of UFO Experiences," *Abducted! Confrontations with Beings from Outer Space,* Coral E. & J. Lorenzen, New York, NY: Berkeley Press, 1977, 191-222.

___"Observations and Conclusions Regarding the Investigation of the UFO Experience of Ms. Smith, Ms. Stafford, and Ms. Thomas," *Situation Red, the UFO Siege!* L.A. Stringfield, Garden City, NY: Doubleday, 1977, 216-221.

_"Investigation of the Alleged UFO Experience of Carl Higdon," *UFO Phenomena and the Behavioral Scientist,* R.F. Haines (ed.), Metuchen, NJ: Scarecrow Press, 1979, 225-35.

_"Using Hypnosis to Decipher the Contactee 'Message'", *Second Look,* May 1979,10 E. St., SE, Washington, DC 20003, 19-21.

_"What are the Implications of UFO Experiences?" *Journal for UFO Studies,* I (1979), No. 1, 101-109.

_"Using the Pendulum Technique in the Investigation of UFO Experiences," Bologna, Italy: EDITECS, III (1978-79), No. 1, 179-218.

_"Models for UFO Evidence," *APRO Bulletin,* XXVIII, No. 2 (Aug. 1979), 7-8; No. 3, Sept. 1979, 4-5.

_"Levels of Reality and the UFO Display," *APRO Bulletin,* XXVIII. No. 4 (Oct. 1979), 8; No. 5, Nov. 1979, 7-8.

_"Psychical Analysis of UFO Experiences," International Symposium on UFO Research, May 22-25, 1992, Denver, CO.

_"Messages from Space," *Proceedings of the 1st International UFO Congress,* C.G. Fuller, (ed.), New York, NY: Warner Books, 1980, 295- 304.

_"Position Statement: UFO Phenomena," *The Encyclopedia of UFOs,* R.D. Story, (ed.), Garden City, NJ: Doubleday, 1980, 348-349.

_"Uses of Hypnosis in UPO Investigation," *The Encydopedia of UFOs,* RD. Story, (ed.), Garden City, NJ: Doubleday, 1980, 180-181.

Top Ten Required Reading

Fowler, R. L. *The Andreasson Affair.* Englewood Cliffs, NJ: Prentice-Hall, 1979.

Fuller, J. G. *The Interrupted Journey.* New York, NY: Dell, 1969.

Haines, R. F. (ed.) *UFO Phenomena and the Behavioral Scientist.* Metuchen, NJ: Scarecrow Press, 1979.

Jung, C.G. *Flying Saucers: A Modern Myth of Things Seen in the Sky.* New York, NY: Signet Books, 1969.

Lorenzen, Coral and Jim: *Abducted! Confrontations with Beings From Outer Space.* New York, NY: Berkley Press, 1977.

Meier, Eduard A. "Billy"; Rashid, Isa; Ziegler, J.H.; and Greene, B.L. (translators). *The Talmud of Jmmanuel: The Clear Translation in English and German.* Tigard, OR: Wild Flower Press, 1992.

National Enquirer UFO Report. New York, NY: Pocket Books, 1985.

Rogo, D. Scott. (ed.) *UFO Abductions.* New York, NY: New American Library, 1980.

Story, R. D. *The Encyclopedia of UFOs.* Garden City, NY: Doubleday Doran. 1980.

Vallee, Jacques. *The Invisible College.* New York, NY: E.P Dutton and Co., 1975.

Topical Bibliography
UFOs and Flying Saucers

Andrews, George. *ExtraTerrestrials Among Us.* St. Paul, MN: Llewellyn, 1986.

Bender, Albert K. *The Case for the UFO.* Clarksburg, PA Saucerian Press.

Binder, Otto. *What We Really Know About Flying Saucers.* New York, NY: Fawcett Publications, 1967.

Blumrich, Josef F. *The Spaceships of Ezekial.* New York, NY: Bantam Books, 1974.

Bowen, Charles. *Encounter Cases from Flying Saucer Review.* New York, NY: New American Library.

Bryant, Alice and Seebach, Linda. *Healing Shattered Reality: Understanding Contactee Trauma.* Tigard, OR: Wild Flower Press. 1991.

Charroux, Robert. *Masters of the World.* New York, NY: Berkley Medallion, 1974.

Davenport, Marc. *Visitors from Time: The Secret of the UFOs.* Tigard, OR: Wild Flower Press, 1992.

Downing, Barry H. *The Bible and Flying Saucers.* New York, NY: Avon, 1970.

Drake, Raymond W. *Cods and Spacemen Throughout History.* Chicago, IL: Henry Regneiy Co., 1975.

Edwards, Frank. *Flying Saucers Here and Now.* New York, NY: Bantam Books, 1968.

Elders, Lee J. (ed.) et al. *UFO Contact From the Pleiades. Vols. I and II.* Text Supervised by Lt. Col. Wendelle C. Stevens. Phoenix, AZ: Genesis III Productions, Ltd., 1980.

Fawcett, Lawrence and Greenwood, Barry. *Clear Intent* Englewood Cliffs, NJ: Prentice Hall, 1984.

Flying Saucers, Serious Business. New York. NY: Bantam Books 1966.

Fowler, Raymond E. *UFOs Interplanetary Visitors.* Englewood Cliffs, NJ: Prentice Hall, 1974.

_*The Andreasson Affair.* Englewood Cliffs, NJ: Prentice Hall, 1979.

Fuller, John G. *Incident at Exeter.* New York, NY: Berkley Medallion, 1969.

_*Interrupted Journey,* New York, NY: Dell, 1969.

Fuller, Curtis G. (ed.) *Proceedings of the First International UFO Congress.* New York, NY: Warner Books, 1980.

Good, Timothy. *Above Top Secret.* New York, NY: William Morrow, 1988.

Haines, Dr. Richard F. (ed.) *UFO Phenomena and the Behavioral Scientist.* Metuchen NJ: Scarecrow Press, 1979.

Hall, Richard. *Uninvited Guests.* Santa Fe, NM:Aurora Press, 1988.

Hendry, Allan. *The UFO Handbook.* Garden City, NY: Doubleday and Co., 1979.

Hobana, Ian and Weverbergh, Juan. *UFOs From Behind The Iron Curtain.* New York, NY: Bantam Books, 1975.

Hopkins, Budd. *Intruders.* New York, NY: Random House, 1987.

Hynek, J. Allen. *The UFO Experience.* New York, NY: Ballantine 1974.

Jung, Dr. Carl G. *Flying Saucers: A Modern Myth of Things Seen in the Sky.* New York, NY: New American Library, 1974.

Kannenberg, Ida. *The Alien Book of Truth.* Tigard, OR: Wild Flower Press, 1992.

Keyhoe, Major Donald E. *Aliens from Space.* New York, NY: New American Library 1974.

_*Flying Saucer Conspiracy.* New York, NY: Henry Holt & Co.,1953

_*Flying Saucers Are Real.* New York, NY: Fawcett, 1950.

Kinder, Gary. *Light Years.* New York: Atlantic Monthly Press, 1989.

Lorenzen, Coral and Jim. *Flying Saucer Occupants.* New York, NY: New American Library, 1968.

_UFOs, The Whole Story. New York, NY: New American Library, 1969.

_Abducted! Confrontations with Beings From Outer Space. New York, NY: Berkley Press, 1977.

Lorenzen, Coral E. Startling Evidence. New York, NY: New American Library, 1966.

Meier, Eduard A. "Billy"; Rashid, Isa; Ziegler, J.H.; and Greene, B.L.(translators). The Talmud of Jmmanuel: The Clear Translation in English and German. Tigard, OR: Wild Flower Press, 1992.

Montgomery, Ruth. Aliens Among Us. New York, NY: G.P Putnam's Sons, 1985.

Mooney, Richard E. Colony Earth. Greenwich, CN: Fawcett Crest Book, 1975.

National Enquirer UFO Report. New York, NY: Pocket Books, 1985.

Raphael. Starseed Transmissions. Kansas City, MO: Uni-Sun, 1982.

Rogo, D. Scott, (ed.) UFO Abductions. New York, NY: New American Library, 1980.

Ruppelt, Edward J. Report on Unidentified Flying Objects. Garden City, NY: Doubleday and Doran, 1956.

Sagan, Carl and Thorton, Page. UFOs: A Scientific Debate. New York, NY: Norton Library, 1974.

Sifkas, Carl. Official Guide to UFO Sightings. New York, NY: Sterling Publications. Co., 1979.

Slater, Philip. The Wayward Gate. Boston: Beacon Press, 1972.

Smith,Warren. The Book of Encounters. New York, NY: Kensington Publications Co., 1976.

Steiger,Brad. Alien Meetings. New York, NY: Ace, 1978.

_Gods of Aquarius. New York, NY: Harcourt, Brace, Jovanovich, 1976.

_and Whritenour, Joan. The New UFO Breakthrough (The Allende Letters). New York, NY: Award Books, 1968.

_(ed). Project Blue Book, New York, NY: Ballantine Books, 1976.

Story, R.D. *The Encyclopedia of UFOs.* Garden City, NY: Doubleday Doran, 1980.

Strieber, Whitley. *Communion.* New York, NY: William. Morrow, 1987.

_*Transformation.* New York, NY: William. Morrow, 1988.

Tomas, Andrew. *We Are Not the First* New York, NY: Ace Books, 1966.

Trench, Brinsley Le Poir. *The Flying Saucer Story.* New York, NY: Ace Books, 1966.

_*The UFO Story—Mysterious Visitors.* Briarcliff Manor, NY: Stein and Day, 1973.

_(ed). *World Round-up of UFO Sightings and Events.* Secaucus, NY: The Citadel Press, 1958.

UFOs Over the Americas. New York, NY: New American Library, 1968.

Vallee, Jacques. *Anatomy of a Phenomenon.* New York, NY: Ace Books, 1965.

_*Challenge to Science: the UFO Enigma.* Chicago, IL: Henry Regnery, 1966.

_*The Invisible College.* New York, NY: E.P Dutton and Co., 1975.

_*Messengers of Deception.* Berkeley, CA: And/Or Press, 1979.

_*Passport to Magonia.* Chicago, IL: Henry Regneiy, 1969.

_*Dimensions.* Chicago, IL: Contemporary, 1988.

_*Confrontations.* New York, NY: Ballantine, 1990.

Weldon, John and Levitt, Zola. *Encounters With UFOs.* Montreal, Canada: Harvest House, 1975.

Wilson, Dr. Clifford. *UFOs and Their Mission Impossible.* New York, NY: New American Library, 1975.

Young, Mort. *UFO Top Secret.* New York, NY: Essandess Special Editions, 1967.

Atlantis

Cayce, Edgar. *Edgar Cayce on Atlantis.* New York, NY: Paperback Library, 1968.

Atlantis, Fact or Fiction? Virginia Beach, VA A.R.E. Press, 1962.

Donnelly, Ignatius. *The Destruction of Atlantis.* Blauvelt, NY: Multi-media Press, 1971.

Ebon, Martin. *Atlantis, The New Evidence.* New York, NY: New American Library, 1977.

Muck, Otto. *The Secrets of Atlantis.* New York, NY: Pocket Books, 1976.

Oliver, F.S. *Phylos the Tibetan: A Dweller on Two Planets,* (written in 1883.) Blauvelt, NY: Multimedia Press, 1974.

Smith, Warren. *Myths and Mysteries of Atlantis.* New York, NY: Kensington, 1975.

Stacy-Judd, Robert B. *Atlantis, Mother of Empires.* Santa Monica, CA: DeVorss & Co., 1939.

Steiger, Brad. *Atlantis Rising.* New York, NY: Dell, 1973.

Zink, Dr. Davi. *The Stones of Atlantis.* Englewood Cliffs, NJ: Prentice Hall, 1978.

Psychic Phenomena

Allen, Maurice. Our *Invisible Friends.* New York, NY: Liveright Publications. Co., 1943.

Ebon, Martin (Ed.) *Parapsychology.* New York, NY: New American Library, 1978.

_(Ed.) *The Psychic Scene.* New York, NY: New American Library, 1974.

Hansel, C.E.M. *ESP Scientific Evaluation.* New York, NY: Charles Scribner's Sons, 1966.

Hudson, Thomas J., Ph.D. *The Law of Psychic Phenomenon.* New York, NY: Kensington Publications Co., 1977.

Mooney, Robert A. *Journeys Out of the Body.* Garden City, NY: Doubleday Co., 1971.

Muldoon, Sylvan and Carrington, Hereward. *Phenomenon of Astral Projection.* New York, NY: Samuel Weiser, 1974.

_Projection of the Astral Body.* New York, NY: Samuel Weiser, 1970.

Ostrander, Sheila and Schroeder, Lynn. *Psychic Discoveries Behind the Iron Curtain.* New York, NY: Bantam Books, 1970.

_ The ESP Papers. New York, NY: Bantam Books, 1976.

Puharich, Andrija. Uri: A Journal of the Mystery of Uri Geller. New York, NY: Bantam Books, 1975.

Smith, Suzy: The Enigma of Out of Body Travel. New York, NY: New American Library, 1968.

_ E.S.P. New York, NY: Pyramid Public, 1962.

Snow, Dr. Chet, and Wambach, Dr Helen. Mass Dreams of the Future. New York, NY: McGraw Hill, 1989.

Stearn, Jess. Adventures into the Psychic. New York, NY: Coward McCann, Inc., 1969.

White, Stewart Edward. Across the Unknown New York, NY: E.P Dutton, 1939.

_ The Betty Book. New York, NY: E.P. Dutton, 1937.

_ The Road I Know. New York, NY: E.P. Dutton, 1942.

_ The Unobstructed Universe. New York, NY: E.P. Dutton, 1940.

Reincarnation

Banjerjee, Dr. H.N. The Once and Future Life. New York, NY: Dell, 1979.

Deardorff, Dr. James W. Celestial Teachings: The Emergence of the True Testament of Jmmanuel (Jesus). Tigard, OR Wild Flower Press, 1991.

Ebon, Martin. Evidence for Life After Death. New York, NY: New American Library, 1978.

Kelsey, Denys and Grant, Joan. Many Lifetimes. Garden City, NY: Doubleday and Co., 1967.

Moody, Raymond A. Jr. (M.D.). Life After Life. New York, NY: Bantam Books, 1976.

Pike, James A. The Other Side. New York, NY: Dell, 1968.

Smith, Alson J. Immortality, the Scientific Evidence. Englewood Cliffs, NJ: Prentice Hall, 1954.

Steiger, Brad and Wiluams, Loring G. Other Lives. New York, NY: Award Books, 1969.

Ancient Civilizations

Budge, E.A. Wallis. *Egyptian Book of the Dead.* New York, NY: Dover Publications. Co., 1967.

Casson, Lionel. *Ancient Egypt.* Alexandria, VA: Time-Life Books, 1965.

Charroux, Robert. *The Mysterious Past.* New York, NY: Berkley Medallion, 1975.

_ *The Mysteries of the Andes.* New York, NY: Avon, 1974.

Churchward James. *The Lost Continent of Mu.* New York, NY: Bro Life, 1991.

deCamp, L. Sprague. *Lost Continents.* New York, NY: Cover Publications, 1970.

Evans-Wentz. *The Tibetan Book of the Dead.* London, England: Oxford University Press, 1960.

Furneaux, Rupert. *Ancient Mysteries.* New York, NY: Ballantine, 1978.

Hawkins, Jacquetta. *Atlas of Ancient Archaeology.* New York, NY: McGraw Hill, 1974.

Horizon Magazine Editors. *Horizon Book of Lost Worlds.* New York, NY: American Heritage Publications Co., 1962.

Hutin, Serge. *Alien Races and Fantastic Civilizations.* New York, NY: Berkley Medallion, 1975.

Krupp, Dr. E.C. *In Search of Ancient Astronomies.* New York, NY: McGraw Hill, 1979.

Landsburg, Alan and Sally. *In Search of Ancient Mysteries.* New York, NY: Bantam Books, 1974.

Lehner, Mark. *The Egyptian Heritage.* Based on Edgar Cayce Readings, Virginia Beach, VA: A.R.E. Press, 1974.

Schwartz, Stephan A. *The Secret Vaults of Time.* New York, NY: Grosset and Dunlap.

Umland, Craig and Eric. *Mysteries of the Ancients.* New York, NY: Walker Publications Co., 1974.

Verrill, A. Hyatt and Ruth. *America's Ancient Civilizations.* New York, NY: G.P. Putnam's Sons, 1955.

von Hassler, Gerd. Translated by Ebon, Martin. *Lost Survivors of the Deluge.* New York, NY: New American Library, 1978.

Williamson, George Hunt. *Secret Places of the Lion.* New York, NY: Warner Commuications, 1958.

Outer Space

Asimov, Isaac. *Extraterrestrial Civilizations.* New York. NY: Crown Publications, 1979.

Blum, Ralph and Judy. *Beyond Earth.* New York, NY: Bantam Books, 1974.

Chatelaine, Maurice. *Our Ancestors Came from Outer Space.* New York, NY: Dell. 1979.

Christian, James L. (Ed.) *Extraterrestrial Intelligence.* New York, NY: Prometheus Books, 1976.

Flindt, Max H. & Binder, Otto. *Mankind, Child of the Stars.* New York, NY: Fawcett, 1974.

Landsburg, Alan and Sally. *The Outer Space Connection.* New York,

NY: Bantam Books, 1975.

Sendy, Jean. *The Coming of the Gods.* New York, NY: Berkley Medallion, 1973.

Sitchin, Zecharia. *The Twelfth Planet* New York, NY: Avon, 1976.

Related Topics

Blavatsky, Madame Helen P. *The Secret Doctrine* (Abridged). Wheaton, IL: Theosophical Publishing House, 1966.

Castaneda, Carlos. *Tales of Power.* New York, NY: Simon and Schuster, 1974.

Clark, R.T. Rundle. *Myth and Symbol of Ancient Egypt.* London, England: Thames and Hudson, 1959.

Cox, J. Halley and Stasack, Edward. *Hawaiian Petroglyphs.* Honolulu, HI: Bishop Museum, 1970.

Eliade, Mircea. *Rites and Symbols of Initiation.* New York, NY: Harper and Row, 1958.

Findhorn Community: *Findhom Garden.* New York, NY: Harper and Row, 1975.

Jeffrey, Adi Kant Thomas. *Parallel Universe.* New York, NY: Warner Books, 1977.

Jung, Dr. Carl G. and M.L. Von Franz. (Eds.) *Man and His Symbols.* Garden City, NY: Doubleday and Co., 1964.

Martineau, La Van. *The Rocks Begin to Speak.* Las Vegas, NV: K.C. Publications, 1973.

McBride, L.R *Petroglyphs of Hawaii* Hilo, HI: The Petroglyph Press Ltd., 1969.

Moore, William. *The Philadelphia Experiment.* New York, NY: Fawcett, 1980.

Nicholson, Irene. *Mexican and Central American Mythology.* London, England: Paul Hamlyn, 1967.

Noorbergen, Rene. *Secrets of the Lost Races.* New York, NY: Harper and Row, 1977.

Pauwels, Louis and Bergier, Jacques. *The Eternal Man.* New York, NY: Avon, 1972.

Prabhupada, (Swami). *Bhagavad Gita As It Is* (Abridged). New York, NY: Bhaktivedanta Book Trust, 1968.

Rhine, J.B. *The Reach of the Mind.* New York, NY: William Sloane Publications, 1974.

Roberts, Jane. *Seth Speaks.* Englewood Cliffs, NJ: Prentice Hall, 1972.

Robinson, Lytle. *Edgar Cayce's Story of the Origin and Destiny of Man.* New York, NY: Berkley Medallion, 1976.

Sanderson, Ivan T. *Abominable Snowmen : Legend Come To Life.* Philadelphia, PA Chilton, 1961.

Steiger, Brad. *Mysteries of Time and Space.* New York, NY: Dell, 1976.

Steiner, Rudolf. *Egyptian Myths and Mysteries.* Spring Valley, NY: Anthroposophic Press, 1971.

Veer, M.H.J. Th. Van der. *Hidden Worlds: Hidden Clues to the Past.* New York, NY: Bantam Books, 1975.

Watson, Lyal. *Gift of Unknown Things.* New York, NY: Simon and Schuster, 1977.

Weed, Joseph J. *Wisdom of the Mystic Masters.* New York, NY: Parker Publications Co., 1968.

White, John. (Eds). *Other Worlds, Other Universes.* Garden City, NY: Doubleday and Co., 1975.

Wilgus, Neal. *The Illuminoids.* New York, NY: Pocket Books, 1979.

Wilson, Colin. *Mysteries.* New York, NY: Perigree Books (Putnam's), 1978.

Ida M. Kannenberg

A pioneer researcher of the UFO enigma, Ida Kannenberg sponsored with Dr. Leo Sprinkle the First Rocky Mountain UFO Conference in 1980 at the University of Wyoming. At the historic conference, she introduced the time travelers that contacted her in 1940.

"Like most UFO abductees or contactees, she [Kannenberg] sees herself as an unobtrusive, unimportant, 'everyday person,'" wrote Dr. Leo Sprinkle. Kannenberg wrote about UFO encounters as she experienced them, information conveyed by the time travelers, and observations about them. She puzzled over composite human nature, humanity as a species, how the species came to its present evolution, and the individual as an existential filament of physical and spiritual worlds. Yet, Kannenberg puzzled in down-to-earth terms and called herself a little old lady in tennis shoes. She extended a steady hand in support of fellow contactees and abductees, and her first book was a manual for UFO experiencers.

A tireless researcher, she wrote seven books about UFO contact, psychic development, ultraterrestrials, extraterrestrials and time travelers. Her books include *UFO Initiation: Ultraterrestrial Time Travelers*; *Project Earth from the ET Perspective: Mind and Species*; *Time Travelers from Atlantis*; *My Brother Is a Hairy Man: The Search for Bigfoot*, *A Son of Old Atlantis*; *Reconciliation*; and *The Alien Book of Truth*.

Ida Kannenberg was born October 27, 1914 in Iowa. She passed from this world on May 17, 2010.

Made in the USA
Middletown, DE
15 April 2022